THE COMBINATION

Other books from the Neighborhood Story Project

Before and After North Dorgenois by Ebony Bolding
Between Piety and Desire by Arlet and Sam Wylie
Palmyra Street by Jana Dennis
What Would the World be Without Women? by Waukesha Jackson

Series Editor: Rachel Breunlin
Graphic Designer: Gareth Breunlin

The Combination
ISBN 1-933368-28-4
ISBN-13 978-1933-36828-3

© 2005 by the Neighborhood Story Project

Let us hear from you. www.neighborhoodstoryproject.org.
Neighborhood Story Project
P.O. Box 19742
New Orleans, LA 70179

Soft Skull Press, Inc.
55 Washington St, Suite 804
Brooklyn NY 11201
www.softskull.com

Distributed by Publishers Group West
www.pgw.com

Text pages produced on 70 lb. Lynx Opaque, Smooth Finish,
donated by Weyerhaeuser Company, Fort Mill, South Carolina
Tango Coated Cover, donated by MeadWestvaco, Stamford,
Connecticut, manufactured in Covington, Virginia
Printing and binding donated by WORZALLA, Stevens Point,
Wisconsin USA

by Ashley Nelson

THE COMBINATION

Neighborhood Story Project
Red Rattle Books/Soft Skull Press
New Orleans, Louisiana
Brooklyn New York
2005

OUR HOME

You look at the ghetto and you see a mess,
We live in the ghetto and we see the best.
The ghetto isn't always drug deals and gunfights,
Most days it's parties, DJ's and sunlight.
Where else on earth you gonna see two black children,
Standing up talking about how to make their first million.
To fix up their home while discovering the truth,
They might leave the hood but they won't forget their roots.
Believe me, making it big doesn't mean you forget your past,
It just means the struggle is changing from bad.
Africa is our heritage, where we were stripped away,
To work in America, but never lead the way.
So we took our pain for all those years
Cried a few nights and shed a few tears.
But we still stood up and came together as people,
United is together, but it doesn't mean equal.
We have done so much yet have nothing to show,
But a nine to five job and an apartment in the ghetto.
But it's ok that we reach with the wrong-colored hand,
Deep in our hearts we know Africa's our homeland
But the ghetto is where we all can stand strong man.

TABLE OF CONTENTS

DEDICATION

I DEDICATE MY BOOK TO LAFITTE AND MY MOM, BOTH OF WHOM I LOVE DEARLY.

ACKNOWLEDGEMENTS

Thank-you first to God and my mom both of whom gave me life, blessings, and love.

Thank-you to my father. I know we don't have a perfect relationship, but we are trying and that's what kept my head up while writing this book.

Thanks to my family: Willie, Keitra, Domonique, Mikky, Bigman, Nuder, Jenny, Anthony, Grandma Pearl, and Uncle Michelle (esp. for the title suggestion). You supported me in any way possible while writing this book.

Abram and Rachel, thanks for making sure I got down to business. You saw something in me and believed. No one's ever done that for me. Rachel, thanks for helping to take pictures and edit the interviews. Y'all my dogs and I love y'all.

Thanks to everyone who was in the Neighborhood Story Project with me: Kesha, Ebony, Jana, Sam, Arlet, Ceirod, and all who made writing a book so damn fun. We had lots of laughs. Thanks y'all.

Thanks to my friends Smitty, Roger, Shykera, Phylicia, Jessica, Sachell, Hope, Brittany, Laronda, my Luther's crew, Milissa, Cookie, and my bestest friendisist, in the whole wide worldesist, Sarah. Most didn't know I was writing a book, but when I told them, they were really happy for me.

Thanks to everyone in Lafitte, especially Pat and Jackie Fulford, Charmaine Williams, Wanda Dubuse, Hope Bland, the women involved in the Residential Council, Fadi Abu Ali, (aka Mike from Busy Bee), Leah Chase, Freeman Louis, Clyde Smith, Dorothy Grace, and Poppee. Without your voices, there wouldn't be a story.

Thanks to everyone who believed enough to give money to support our project and keep it going. You saw us and our talent—thank you for believing.

Thank-you to all the people I've looked to throughout my life because without them I wouldn't have ambition: Tupac, Omar Tyrese, Oprah, Bob Marley, Malcolm X, MLK, Alice Walker, Styles P, DMX, Nas, Jay AZ, Biggie, Big Pun, TLC, Alicia Keys, Michael Jackson, Janet Jackson, Jadda Kiss, Samuel L. Jackson, John Travolta, the writers of *Chicken Soup for the Teenage Soul*, Rosa Parks, Tyler Perry, TD Jakes, Kimberly Elise, and the whole Set If Off crew.

Thank-you also to my haters I did it all for you. Ha! Ha!

If I forgot anyone this last ones for you. Thanks to everyone who was a part of this project and believed because that's all we needed—someone to believe.

INTRODUCTION

If I could pick anyone to read my book, I think it would be my mom and my neighborhood, because they are my book. Every page and every story I wrote was for them. My mom always told me to be happy, you got to do what makes you happy, and for me that means writing. She would've been so happy to see this book because she always believed in me.

The Lafitte Public Housing Development on Orleans Avenue in the Sixth Ward is a combination of friends, family, support, and love, but it's also a place where a lot of people are scared to go. I wonder if they're scared of us and that's why they are afraid to spend time there, or maybe it's because our buildings aren't as beautified as other neighborhoods. Either way, you wouldn't see someone from the suburbs just walking through saying, "Oh, I was just in the neighborhood, thought I'd swing by." We do have problems in Lafitte, but damn, it doesn't mean you have to run away from us. The world has problems and we are all a part of them somehow, even if people don't want to admit it.

Lafitte is the neighborhood I grew up in. It's the place where I went through a lot of different struggles in both my family and the larger community, but it's also the place where I learned about caring. As I began to write my book, I wanted to include stories that showed that Lafitte is a combination of both good and bad. The people know how to make it through the worst and still love where they come from. My mom got caught up in the bad part—the part that outsiders use to label the whole community. I used to get mad at her because I knew she was too smart for that. At first, I was afraid to write about my mom because I didn't want people to judge her or me. But as I wrote about the neighborhood, it was impossible for me not to write about her. I realized she is a part of the combination that is Lafitte.

I struggled most days I had to write because I had to put true emotion into my stories. Don't get me wrong: I love my book and my struggles because they remind me that I did it. Oh God, I did it!! Sorry, I am excited. When you read this book don't feel sorry for me because I don't need it. I am in a place now that I feel comfortable sharing my memories. I've grown up, been through the worst and back, and still doing me and taking care of the family. Pity is the last thing I need. Ya know what? If you feel me, figure out your own combination and unlock the world.

PART I: FAMILY

This part introduces you to my family—the people who raised me and grew up with me in Lafitte. We lived on Orleans Avenue upstairs from my grandma. Eight kids and two parents: we ran between apartments, across the street to the corner stores, and around the cuts and driveways.

We traveled through the good times and the bad, the fights and the make-ups. As we grew up, we knew we had each other, but it didn't help us escape from loneliness all the time. And although we moved in and out of the project, I always felt like Lafitte was my home.

MEET MY MOM

My mother's name was Jalna Nelson and despite the drugs, the cries, and all the broken promises she was still a good person. I remember what she was like before she would smoke the drugs. She was a mother, a mother with all the love that a mother who didn't use would have. Drugs changed her. Every time she was high, drugs made my mother forget she loved us so she did things that she normally wouldn't. But I forgave and loved her even if she forgot she loved me. The way I saw it was, "That high woman isn't my mom. The woman deep down inside her is, and that's who I loved."

My mother and I were close—in fact, very close. We always talked about the ways of life and the power of a choice. My mother told me once she wished she never had kids so we wouldn't have had to go through so much. It didn't make me sad, it made me wish I wasn't born only so she could be happy because her happiness meant a lot to me.

MEET MY DAD

The first time I met my father, Darren Williams, was at my mom's funeral. I had lived with him and my mom since birth but I never knew him. He is a very secretive person, but I think that's only to us. I don't know much about him because when I was young he never talked to us. He would come home from work and just go to his room. When I was young I feared him, not because he physically hurt us, but because I didn't know him as a person—all I knew was that he was my father.

At my mother's funeral, he truly acted as a father. We were sitting in a black limousine on the way home from the cemetery and he told us it would be okay because he'd take care of us. And he does. We live with him and he tries to be a good parent. I know it's hard because he misses Mom. He wears their engagement rings on a necklace. It makes me sad inside that he's like this locked door with no key. Despite it, I still love him.

MEET MY PARENTS

My mom graduated from John McDonogh at the top of her class and then attended community college before working at City Hall. My father graduated from Joseph S. Clark and was one step from being a cop, but then changed his mind. I loved to hear my mama tell the story of how they got together. He was working as a deliveryman and used to deliver packages to City Hall. My mama was a frequent topic of conversation amongst his co-workers. Slim and dark-skinned, my mama explained, "I was a stallion." My daddy and his co-workers made a bet over who could get a date with my mama. Being the scam artist that he is, my daddy told her what the bet was about and proposed that they pretend be going out together and split the money. "Fifty-fifty," she said, "cuz I don't play that." They wound up falling for each other anyway.

My mother and father were together for years. They seemed so happy at times. I mean, we did lots of family things together like going to City Park on weekends to feed the ducks or sometimes we'd all sit in the living room and play board games.

My mom enjoyed cooking and was a pro at it. She always wanted us to learn to cook. She used to buy French bread and make us crumble it up for bread pudding. It was delicious. She also made candy apples and donuts for us. We'd all sit in the living room and watch a movie. My dad is a good cook, too. Mom used to let him cook the red beans on Sundays because she said he made them best. Every Christmas and Thanksgiving they both would make a feast: six or seven sweet potato pies, turkey, ham, potato salad, macaroni and cheese, dressing, baked cakes and more.

My mom was a great swimmer. In summer, I would go with Domonique, Anthony, Mikky, and sometimes Bigman to Tremé or Starling to swim. One evening, we went to Starling and my mom, Jenny, and Nuder were already there. We had so much fun. After we left the pool we went to the store and my mom bought us junk food.

My dad didn't do things like that on his own. The fun times I remember with my dad, my mom was there, too. On Easter, they'd wake us early so we could dye eggs and make baskets. My mom and dad both were Catholic so afterwards we'd go to church St. Peter Claver, which wasn't too bad. On regular days, my dad did simple things like wrestle with us or crack jokes. I do remember my dad combing my hair one time. I think I was about seven years old. My mom must have been gone. I can't really remember but I know it was very pretty and I was grateful.

My father did drugs first. He introduced them to my mom when my brothers and sister and I were young. They used to be in the kitchen with a curtain hanging up. That stanky smell would drift into the living room and we used to get all dizzy off the contact. Sometimes they used to lock us in our room so we wouldn't be near it. In that locked room, we'd all have long talks about our dreams and wishes. I can honestly say that they were all the same—to be happy with mama and daddy.

My mom and dad used heavy. My mom would leave for three and four days at a time—God, I missed her so much—and when she'd come home, we wouldn't be angry. We'd all run over and give her a hug because we missed her. My dad would come in from work, see her gone and leave, too. All we would have was each other.

My father quit long before my mom. His willpower must've been stronger than hers because she kept using and hurting us. I don't think she knew how much I cried when she would leave. At night, I prayed she'd quit but she never did, so then I started praying for her to be safe. I never blamed anyone for my parents or for my life because I looked at it like this: "The rain will soon by over." Who'd ever thought it would've ended the way it did?

WE ARE ALL WE REALLY HAVE

2416 Orleans Avenue is where my siblings and I grew up. We lived in a two bed-room project with nothing but each other. Five girls and three boys. The oldest two didn't live there all the time because they had family on their fathers' sides who they'd stay with from time to time.

Willie is my mother's first son. He's the oldest out of all of us. I don't really remember too much of Willie being home when I was young because he ran away a lot. I guess he couldn't deal with mom's problem and how it caused us to live lonely and scared. I know deep down wherever he went on those nights he still felt that loneliness. When he was home he was a normal boy—cracked jokes on his sisters.

Willie and I were always close. At my mom's funeral, I remember crying non-stop and I also remember Willie being the one patting my back. People always judge him as a thug and don't believe how intelligent he is until they talk to him. We've always had great conversations, especially about religion. Willie says the pope's evil. He's the reason I read the chapter of Revelation in the Bible. He told me, "It'll help you understand things better." What it did was scare me half to death and make mme think the devil was always watching. I forgave him for that and just kept on, still a little shaky though.

Keitra is my oldest sista. She as an attitude outta this world. People who know her always ask, "Wuz she always like that?" I always answer that question by just responding, "Like what? She's nice to me."

Domonique and I were in the middle. When we were young, Domonique was the cool one. She had all the friends and fame at school and in the project. Dominique is a leader. She wouldn't be right for any other title.

She was my competition as a child. We never got along. I guess it was because we are the same in many ways. Though we have our differences, the things we have in common stand out. She's the reason I got into poetry—wanting to do what she did. Domonique is the freestyle princess. Give her a track and there is no doubt she won't rip it. She's good. I mean, really good.

Darren and Mikael are next. We call them Big Man and Mikky. They are so very different. Big-man makes good grades, does half of what he supposed to do and loves games like Playstation, 64, and GameCube.

Mikky stays outside more. He has got to be the most daring person I know. When we were young, he did the wildest shit you can name like seeing a lil' girl on a new bike and just taking her off it or going in a grocery store, filling a basket with junk food and just pushing it out of the store. He had this whole "fuck the world" thing going on and did what he pleased. Mikky never went to school and if he did, he was getting sent home for behavior.

Last but not least is Jahntrell and Iesha who are known to all as Jenny and Nuder—my two youngest sisters who I can't get to understand the words: "Stop touching my stuff." Jenny is my fourteen year old hairstylist. She does all sorts of styles and has never been to hair or beauty college. A lot of people think we look alike because we both have light brown eyes, which is true: we're sisters, of course we're going to look alike! I told my dad that he should let her attend John Mac because they have a great cosmetology department, but he, along with others, thinks John Mac is a school for idiots. Thanks to my dad, Jenny is a spoiled child. She get what she wants from him, which isn't a bad thing because the money she makes on hair she can spend on whatever else she wants.

Nuder is my heart. She is my baby sista and my biggest fan. The reason we click so much is because she understands why I write. Nuder was young when my mom was using drugs, but she understood what was happening. We took care of her some of the time because she was so young. When she was about three, we would play baby with her and dress her up as an infant.

I love all my brothers and sisters because if no one knows, they know. They know and understand every smile and every cry in my life because they've had the same in theirs. We fuss and fight all the time, but inside we love each other because we are all we really have and ya know what? That's fine by me.

THE CREW

My cousin Anthony was about ten when he moved in the Lafitte. His mom was having problems, so Grandma Pearl took him in. Both of Anthony's parents used drugs so we had a lot in common and about the same amount of disappointments. Domonique, Anthony, and I were less than a year apart. With Mikky, we formed a little crew.

Domonique always had to be in charge, no matter who she had to jab (and you better believe she woulda jabbed yo ass.) If you disagreed with her she'd say, "Go your own way then." Anthony was always Domonique's partner like Batman and Robin, Tom and Jerry, and Ren and Stimpy—they were tight like that. Anthony knew his role and played it well. He was Domonique's right hand man, but not too much like her. He's always playing some kind of joke on you, or setting you up for a fall, which made Domonique laugh so she kept him close. One thing I love about Anthony is his respect for women. He's had that since we were young. I guess he got it from growing up around us. I mean, he's a player and all but he's never went as far as calling girls bitches and whores. And that's one of his best qualities.

Mikky did anything without a care in the world and I think that's how he became part of the crew— by not caring. Last but not least was me, who often got kicked out of the clique for not doing something crazy or for not being afraid of Domonique. We always had conflict over simple things like where we were going to go wreak havoc. I remember many fist fights in the driveway over things I don't even remember doing. Domonique used to tell me I thought I was better than everyone, which was so far from the truth. I think that's why she hated me.

There wasn't a lot for kids to do around the projects, so we used to make our own entertainment.

PLAYING "IT" ON THE ROOF OF THE SCRAP YARD

One night after coming back from riding our bikes and jacking other people's, we were chillin in the yard when somebody came up with the idea of playing "It." For those of you who don't know "It" is like a tag game. One person is "it" and if that person touches you, you're it. Simple really, but we were tired of playing in the projects because you can't run around there touching on people so we decided to play at a can recycling company called Southern Scrap. Anyway, the scrap yard is huge. There is plenty of space and places to hide so we all went.

The first run was for Anthony. He didn't mind because he was the fastest out of all of us, but soon the game became boring on the ground. We climbed all the way to the roof of the scrap building, which has to be at least one billion feet in the air. Forgive my fear of heights—about 20 feet high. They played because I wasn't about to break my neck. I'm crazy, but not stupid. I sat at the very top of the roof, which wasn't very smart, but who's judging anyways, while they ran up and down, back and forth, and a little bit in between. Finally, it was time to go but we couldn't just leave. We had to take something or mess something up. That's just what we did. We left them a little surprise. One of the boys knocked down this barrel and about a million cans rolled all over the ground.

We had so much fun on the roof we decided to go again, but we couldn't get in. Because of our lil' message, they put two big dogs in the yard.

MS. PACMAN AT TAYLOR'S

Taylor's was the only store in Lafitte that had an old-timed Ms. PacMan machine with a real joystick. People my age didn't actually come up off Ms. Pac Man—it was before my generation—but it was still influential because it was one of the first video games. I remember many days of waiting for a turn on the game. People would be lined up, damn near around the corner, waiting on food while they played Ms. PacMan. Most people would only get off the machine to get their food or have a friend hold their place. Ms. Ruby would be like, "Y'all's hot sausage po-boy is up." You'd scramble to find someone in the long food stamp line to hold your place while you ran up to the counter. You'd have to dodge the other line of people waiting to snatch your neck off for pausing the machine. They would yell out, "Uh huh. Never no days like that, baby. You gotta play your own turn!"

It was fun to watch the game because you learn off other's mistakes. I played Ms. PacMan all day one time and it kinda paid off because I got in the top 10. I proudly typed in, A S H so people would know it was me, it didn't last long, because the next day I got knocked off by D E E. I never knew who this guy was, but he had the first five spots locked down every time I went there. The glory was fun while it lasted.

MISBELIEVES

The crew loved Misbelieves. The only problem was we could only find them in summer. All year long, we stalked houses in the Sixth Ward with Misbelieve trees, because we didn't have one. We'd wait until they were orange, jump the gate, and attack the tree. Sometimes we were too late and the grown-ups got there first. I remember one particular tree over by Busy Bee's Food Store. We were cool with the owners Mike and Ken. They used to give us Now and Laters when we'd go in to get milk or eggs for my mom. During Misbelieve season, the fruit was better than any candy they could give us. We jumped over their fence to steal them, and Ken came out yelling, "Get y'all's bad ass out da tree!" But the Misbelieves were so good we just came right back two minutes later. When we came back, there was a lock on the gate, but we weren't defeated. We asked this old guy for a hammer so we could break the lock. He told us to follow him. He broke the lock, climbed up the tree and began shaking all the Misbelieves into our bags. When he got down, he said, "Y'all better give me some. I ain't do that for free." And we handed him over a percentage.

DOMONIQUE TO THE RESCUE

There was a time in our lives when we'd play in the park, if it wasn't full of older people drinking and smoking weed. We'd go to a corner store and get candy, walk over to the park and eat it. We would occasionally see who could jump the highest off a moving swing, but mainly we went there to chill.

One particular day, the regular crew was hanging out. Bigman was there as well, which was a huge surprise that Domonique hadn't sent him off for not being down enough. Well, someone came up with the idea of jumping off a slanted roof that had to be nine-feet on one side and six-feet on the other. We all went to the six foot end and looked for a minute. I can't say if their feelings and mine were the same, but I was scared and didn't want to do it. Bigman was the only one smart enough to stay on the ground. Anthony and Mikky jumped first—typical boy thing to show off. They sat on the end and shuffled their bodies off. After they landed, I saw to my horror that Domonique hadn't jumped yet. I looked at her to see if she was waiting for Anthony and Mikky to stop screaming, "JUMP!" but she wasn't. She was really afraid. I felt for her because it was her duty to jump because she was the leader. She sat down, closed her eyes and slid off.

My turn was next and with Domonique on the ground I had to jump. Up until that point, I never understood why at Phyllis Wheatly we took counseling classes once a week to help us deal with peer pressure. God, I wished I would've watched those Fat Albert movies in that class. I stood at the edge and rather than sitting, I jumped. I broke my leg in two places. I remember hitting the ground so hard, I thought I broke a rib. I also remember waking from the daze of the fall to see Domonique—who I thought hated me—reaching out to help me.

GRANDMA PEARL

My grandma, Annie Pearl Nelson, is known to all in Lafitte as Ms. Pearl. When we were growing up, she lived right under us. We stayed at 2416 Orleans and she stayed at 2414.

When I was really little, I stayed with her. I remember times my mom would come over angry and would just take me away. I would cry and cry to go back, not because I didn't like my mom's house but because I missed my grandma. I was always a grandma's girl. I used to lay up under her all the time just to be close. When I was about six or seven years old, she gave me my very first book. It was called *Baby Days*. Every night she would read it to me and I just loved it.

My grandma knew that we were bad-ass kids. There were so many days people came to her door to tell on us for destroying somebody's property or taking it. Anthony lived with her, so he was punished ninety percent of the time. We didn't get punished, and if we did, we snuck outside because we were bad. I liked living next door to my grandma. She always had candy treats or something to munch on. Damn, I miss them days.

Awhile back we used to argue more than normal over things like, "Who's your favorite grandchild?" I wanted to be so badly, but I didn't think I was, so I had a lot of envy and jealousy towards Willie and

Anthony. I grew up to realize that she loves all of us and just because it's not all in the same way does not mean she doesn't.

My grandma believes in me. She saved me from group homes, she gave me a room and fed me her food and for that I will never stop loving her. I want to make my grandma proud of me. She gave me my first book and now she's helping me write one of my own When I asked her about how she felt about me interviewing her, she laughed and said, "Well, Miss Ashley, let me tell you. I know you weren't gonna stop until you jam this stuff out of the way, but I have no problem with anything I can do to help you."

BEGINNINGS

I've always been able to get on. I always find good neighbors. People who look out for each other's kids or if someone is sick, they'll chip in. These kinds of people exist and in the housing developments they exist. People pull together because most everyone knows just about everybody else's situation. You'd be surprised.

My family moved to New Orleans from Mississippi in the late forties. My parents was looking for better jobs. In the city, my father was a longshoreman and my mother was a Coca-Cola bottle inspector.

I was raised up in the French Quarter on Dauphine Street. We would all get up in the morning around seven and go to the bakery and get French bread. Come back, have French bread with hot chocolate or coffee before we'd go to school at Craig Elementary. That's what everyone in the neighborhood did in the morning.

You know know, they had about just as many black and white in the same area. You would think at that time, back in the sixties, all the people would be so segregated. But the white kids and the black kids, they played together outside. They did hopscotch and played jacks. It's not the kids with the segregation, it's the parents. I had a lot of friends on the block and we used to play. We didn't have a doll, so we made our own. We would take ropes and put them in bottles to make a doll and we would comb their hair. That's how I learned how to plait hair.

My first job was as a waitress in McCarter's on Canal Street. McCarter's was a five and ten cent store—something like Woolworth's. They had an area for the blacks and an area for the whites. And in the black area they worked behind the counter, but in the white area they had waitresses on the floor.

With desegregation, they had to put some African-Americans on the floor. I was the first one. All these other people had been there for years and years and years, but they put me out. That's why we figured they expected me to fail, because they knew all these things, and I didn't know them. But the blacks—and they had some whites—were helping. People were getting my orders up, my tables set, and gettin them cleared, and everything, ya know. They didn't want it to be seen, but they were doin it. I had a lot of people workin with me to help me, sayin, "You can't, girl, you can't fail. You got to do this. You know what they're waitin for: 'We tried, but she didn't work out.'"

I had no sisters and brothers, so I followed my parents when they moved to the Ninth Ward. I didn't even have a problem adjusting because I can mostly meet and get along with the average person. Ya know, you may not think of it, but people will give you a welcome when you move into a new area. They'll introduce themselves and see if they can help. Then you get to start knowing everybody in the area. You get to know the good from the bad; you know to stay away from the bad. I haven't had any problems with any neighbors in any area that I lived in.

LAFITTE

I heard about the low-income housing development, so I put in an application and after a few years, I was called and became eligible to move in at Lafitte. I've been living here almost forty years. When I first moved into Lafitte, this was the very best housing development there was. The kids could come outside and they could play. You could leave all the doors and windows open. We didn't have to worry about breakin in, robberies, or anything like this. We didn't have to worry about anyone fightin, coming through shooting. It was just a very nice area.

But now there's drugs back here. But before then, if there were drugs it wasn't in the open, ya know. But now you could see transactions goin on anywhere you might be passin. They're robbin. They're fightin, killin each other, and stealin. It's not even safe with the doors open. I've had someone run in my door twice and the police were there, and they ran in my house twice.

I just gotta be careful and keep my doors locked. I don't fear anyone because I know most of the kids that grew up around here. I know them. They give me a lot of respect; I respect them. The violence is more with the young people. It's not that they're coming after elderly people—breakin in your homes and things. I think my door just happened to be open and this guy was running and he just came in the first door that he saw open. But the police were right behind him and they were going to get him without any problems.

SPEAKING-UP

I think a lot of people don't vote. And then when something go wrong, they're all, "That's not right. You shouldn't do this. And this is what's wrong with it." I feel like if you don't vote, you aren't exercising your voice, and you don't have anything to say. Yesterday I was telling em, "Come on, we goin vote."

"I'm goin."

"No, we goin *now*. If I'm goin, then I know you goin."

So I rounded up some people, and we went to vote. Then I said, "Now you go where you want to go. You did what I wanted." And then there were some people in the line voting, someone was saying, "Oh, I'm twenty-four years old. I'm twenty-seven years old. I'm thirty years old. This is my first time." I said, "You don't worry about it being your first time, you're here, that's all that matters. That you're here today."

GRANDMA LIDDIE

If you knew grease was hot would you touch it? Or if you knew a plane was going to crash would you catch it? No, because you know the outcome of it already. But what if nature makes you forget everything—outcomes, your friends, and even your family? It's hard. My great grandma struggles with this everyday. She has Alzheimer's. She is slowly forgetting who we are and who she is, but we'll never forget. We'll never forget our Grandma Liddie who, if you back talking, gon make you get your own switch for your ass wuppin. She used to tell me "Girl, you are so womanish you stank."

Grandma Liddie is the family. She is the beginning and when I say beginning, I mean she was the first one to move to New Orleans from Mississippi. Since then, we have all been raised in the city: it's her, my grandma, my mom, and finally my generation, which I am so glad she's here to see. I always thought her accent was so funny and she still uses words she grew up on like commode and cap instead of toilet and hat. My great grandma is important to our family. It's hard to have her see me everyday and not remember who I am because if you think about it, our memories are all we truly have. I wonder if it makes her sad that she's lost that part of herself or maybe she doesn't even know. All I know is she hasn't lost her humor or kindness, and those are the parts that I love so much.

WILDIN' OUT

v. 1. Trippin 2. Doing things your way no matter what the consequences

At age thirteen it first began. I began to hate myself and my life. I often cried and asked, "Why am I not loved? Why does my family have to struggle?" And the repeated question, "Where is mom?" I hated living yet I was more afraid of death because where do you go when you die? No one knows, and that is very scary.

It's hard trying to grow in a broken home when the truth is: you never really grow, you only deal. I'd lived through no shoes for school, no food to eat, and no one to hold, and at that stage in my life, I didn't care anymore. I saw the world as this ugly place I had to live in so I began to cut school, fight and lash out at anyone who only wanted to help. I didn't need help. I needed my family. I mean, it's all I ever wanted: a mom, a dad, brothers, and sisters, a lil' dog and a big house like on the Cosby Show. I had raised myself for so long I got the thought in my mind that, "If you not taking care of me, don't tell me what to do."

I always wish things in my life would've ended differently. I know I can't change the past, but I love going back there to a place where my mom never died and my family was sitting in our project living room eating donuts she made out of biscuit dough.

A YEAR AT THE METHODIST HOME

February 14, 2001 was the day of my hearing to see if my attitude had changed since my last hearing for constantly running away and not going to school. Judge Nancy told me that I must go to school or I would be removed from my home and placed in a more strict environment. I took it for a joke and didn't follow any of her instructions. I was told at my second hearing that I would be sent to the Methodist Home for Children until the people in the facility saw fit for me to go home.

Leaving the dim lighted courtroom with two officers—one tall and thick and the other short and slim—I thought to myself, "This is really happening." It was like reality was setting and finally about to reveal the illusion of my fantasy world—the one where I made the rules. We arrived on Washington Avenue to a huge building with so few windows. I stopped and took a very long look because this was it; this would be my life for God-knew-how-long.

I lived down the street from the main building in a big white house with three bedrooms for six girls. It was like your typical first day of school. The one where you worry if you'll be accepted in a clique or will you be as you came—alone. As I walked in,

I was greeted by a slim white girl with brown hair. She introduced herself as Sarah and told me I was her new roommate. She was like the first white girl I had ever really had a conversation with. I think she wanted to be friends from the beginning, but I wasn't interested in making any. She liked pop music and listened to B-97 and I'm a hip-hop and R&B person and listen to Q-93. I didn't think it would work, but she kind of opened my eyes about things because now I listen to both radio stations.

Sarah and I had so much fun together in our room, we swore to be Roommates 4 Ever. Sarah was like my sister: whatever she had, I had; whatever I had, she had. It was just like that between us. She showed me how to apply makeup. She would always make me over. She gave me this hooker look one time. Now, I am not a hooker but I did love the wild woman look. We talked all the time. Some of the best conversations in my life were with her. We'd sit up all night talking, sometimes until we begged each other to shut up but the silence didn't last long. We were back keeping each other awake again.

Sarah had a thing for stuffed animals. She had about a million just on her bed. I remembered her favorite was McGruff—her crime-fighting dog. I would take him and throw him in the living room. Sarah would get so mad, even though she knew it was a joke. Sarah left before me. She went to a foster home. I really, really didn't want her to go, but that would've been selfish of me to ask her to stay and miss the chance to have a family for my benefit.

I was cool with most of the other girls because I understood them. One day Emily, a slim white girl with blond hair, asked me why I was there. I told her from running away. I asked her the same and she said when she was young her mother used to sell her to men. Her mother went to jail because she had been taking pictures of it and putting it on the internet and the police traced it back to her. They sent Emily away.

Other girls had stories that were equally painful. Becky, a slim white girl, was there because she went crazy when her daddy started raping her. She finally told her mama and the police can't find either one of them. Those stories really got to me because I never thought these things actually happened. I thought that was some Lifetime movie network type thing, but it does happen.

The stories of those girls who I knew for about a year changed my life because I had been running away from my family and these kids were trying to find one.

Ashley and Sarah

BAD NEWS

It was June or July when she told us. I can't really remember because I was still in Methodist when I found out and in the home you never know what month it is because they all feel the same. We were all in the visiting room: Dominique, Jenny, Nuder, Bigman, and Mikky. Mama and daddy came to visit us that day. After I was sent to the place I frequently referred to as Hell!!!!, Domonique, Mikky, and Bigman were sent there as well. Mama didn't look well. A couple of weeks back she had a stroke and was just getting the feeling in the left side of her body. She told us that the doctor had given her a CAT scan and her results were back. At that moment, I knew there would be bad news. I had a feeling in my gut and there was. She told us she had a tumor on her brain and had to have surgery. Jenny and Nuder cried out first. They grabbed mom and hugged her tight. Mikky, Domonique, Bigman, and I cried in silence.

I didn't understand what was going on. All that was running through my mind was, "Oh my God, my mom's gonna die," and that feeling I can say was the worst feeling I've ever felt in all the years I've been on this earth. We stayed the whole visit. We tried to laugh and talk but we were all too sad to enjoy anything. My dad looked the worst. I watched him from the corner I sat in as he tried to be strong in front of us. I think my dad loved my mom more than himself. When it came time to leave, we all hugged and went our separate ways.

On our next visit, mama and daddy didn't show, but Nuder and Jenny came. We all just chilled together in silence. Nuder broke it by asking, "Is Mama gonna die?" I think she wanted me to tell her no, but I couldn't tell her anything because I didn't know. Bigman answered, "No, she ain't gon die. She gotta have surgery, then she gon be okay." Jenny asked, "What if the surgery don't work?" I just sat quietly while my sisters and brothers talked about mom. Domonique didn't say anything either; I think she was too sad to speak. They fussed the whole visit and I just sat there with them trying to find answers to the questions spinning around in my head.

THE MAN MY FATHER IS

My mom was sick when I came home. She had an operation and they removed the tumor, but she had another one the doctors had overlooked. It spread to her lungs. She took chemotherapy and radiation that made her vomit and tired all the time. She was weak from the treatments, but still could crack a good joke every now and then. My mom knew she was gonna die and I think that's why she cried a lot in those last months. She became very dependent on her kids— mainly me, which wasn't a problem because she needed me and I was there. We took care of her the best we could, but the doctors said all treatment had failed; there was nothing they could do. But that was bullshit. They did what we could pay for, not all they could do.

One night, my dad called me into the kitchen. He had a little box sitting next to his coffeepot and told me to open it. Inside was a gold ring with diamonds all over. He told me he was gonna ask my mom to marry him. I think that was the first real smile I flashed since the bad news. I told him, "This will make her so happy."

Later that night I was asleep on the side of her bed. My dad came into the room so I played like I wasn't awake because I knew this was the time. He walked over to the opposite side of the bed and bent down to talk to her, but my mom spoke first. She said, "All I want is for you to take care of my children." He responded, "All I want is for you to marry me." She began to cry. She was so emotional her last months but these tears, these were tears of happiness. My mom was really happy and I could tell my dad was, too.

She wore her ring the next morning. She showed me in a bragging type way. I didn't tell her that I already knew. They never married because her condition got worse, but my dad was always by her side— loving her and giving her hope. I never understood my father but as I remember how he was during the time my mom was sick, I understand the man my father is. That type of man is very rare these days: one who is there during the good times and will still be there through the bad ones. One who will love you, always have your hand, and an open arm you can lie in when you feel alone.

ON THAT NIGHT

I cleaned the whole house that day— even the room she was to rest in. She was released from the hospital because she was dying and no one could save her. The doctors sent her home with a bed and lots of morphine to ease the pain. I don't remember what time she came home, but I do know it was dark and some of the family was there—my grandma, Domonique, my dad, and also my Uncles Mitch and Junior. My Uncle Junior's wife came, too. We all stayed in the room talking. We hoped she'd hear and wake up but she just laid in the bed. Every now and then she'd raise her eyes, but the morphine kept her weak. My uncles stayed for an hour or so and then left. It was only Domonique, who was cooking with me in the kitchen, my Grandma who was on her cell phone, and my dad who had locked himself in his room. I had been going to check on her every few seconds since she'd been there and I was on my way again. I guess I kept checking her room because I knew she could go anytime and I didn't want that to happen. I tried to stay close to help if she needed anything or felt any pain.

As I entered the room her eyes were shut. I was so scared. I walked over and she looked up at me. I was so relieved. I could hear the pain in her voice when she asked me to pull her covers up. I kissed her on the cheek and whispered I loved her because I did. I left the room and went to the kitchen to help Domonique finish fixing the food when my grandma yelled, "Go check on ya Mama." I told her, "I just left outta the room a few minutes ago and she was fine."

I still went back to check. This time her eyes were open. I walked over to the bed because I had been standing there at least two minutes and didn't see her blink. When I got over to the bed, I touched her hand. It was cold. I began to shake her body when I realized she wasn't moving at all. I called out for Domonique. My grandma came in the room, too, and together they went towards the bed and I backed into a corner. I knew she was dead, but I ran out of the room and told my dad, "Mom wasn't moving."

He cried before he stood up. He ran into the room and grabbed her. He began to shake her but it was pointless. My grandma couldn't stop crying and Domonique called 911. When the ambulance came they tried to revive her. I couldn't believe it. I just stood in the hallway while people ran back and forth inside the room. They never told us she was dead. They told us they'd bring her to the hospital and see if they could get her breathing again. My grandma told me to stay home while she followed the ambulance with my dad and Domonique.

I was home alone. I went into the room she died in and cried. I was too afraid to touch anything so I sat on the floor or maybe I fell. All I remember was breaking down. My body felt weak and my eyes felt heavy.

I knew there would be pain but damn! It hurt so bad until tears wouldn't even fall. I just screamed. No one was home, so I let it all out. Later Domonique, my dad, and my grandma came home from the hospital all in tears. They decided to tell everyone by my grandma's house so we went there the same night. The house was full, but it seemed to be so empty. Everyone was there, but mom wasn't. I missed her and she was only gone a few hours. I think it was the thought that she was never coming back that made my tears endless.

HELP FROM THE STRANGEST PLACES

I live in what can be considered a community: a bunch of people of all ages living together. Yet people don't call where I live a community; they call it the ghetto. To be honest, for a long time it never felt like a community to me because everyone seemed to fend for themselves and in a community people help one another by doing anything they can to help a neighbor feel comfortable. But I was wrong and I apologize. Although it took me some time to realize it, now I see.

When my mother passed away, it was a hard time for my whole family but I think I took it the hardest. I had what I call a "sometimes" relationship with my mom. Sometimes we got along and sometimes we argued. Thinking back to the bad times, I am sorry I didn't walk away instead of fussing and trying to prove a point when she was right all along. My mom and I talked all the time about boys, sex, drugs—things parents don't usually talk to their kids about. We had an open relationship and I could tell her anything. I think that and seeing her face is what makes me cry at night and makes me miss her so much. Because I really do.

I still remember the day of the funeral. It was cold but I refused to wear a coat. The sky to me looked dark which isn't strange to me at all because everything that day through my eyes looked dark. I cried endless tears that day and questioned God repeatedly, *Why?!* I'd scream on the inside, *Now I have no one. Do you know I have no one?*

At the service, a woman my grandma knew sang. It was so beautiful that everyone cried. My tears were there before the song but you can say the song brought them out.

After the service my family went to my grandma's house to cry, I guess, because that's all I saw — people crying and holding each other. I sat in this blue chair my grandma had since as long as I could remember and put my head in my lap and finished off where I left off at the funeral home. I cried. I cried like a baby in desperate need of a bottle. I cried as if I were a fourteen-year old girl who'd just lost her mother and has no shoulders to lean on, and I had that right, because it was true.

I looked up after hearing noise and it was a bunch of people I've never associated with in my life bringing cold drinks and food, and consoling both my family and me. They offered to help in any way they could and that day, that cold and distant day, I never got to thank those people and let them know how much what they did meant to me. And I know it's been a long time but I haven't forgotten and I really want to say thanks. Hopefully one of you will read my book and see how much you not knowingly touched my heart. Oh! And that help from strange places doesn't seem so strange at all.

SONG TO MAMA

At night I always wish that I could see u again
Cuz you wuz more than a mother, u wuz my best friend
I didn't have an easy life and u can vouch for dat
See, I ain't got much now, but I'll give it all back
To see yo face, smile or a glance from the sun
This is my life story and the chapter's begun
In this life, I then done so many things,
asking for help when I knew I was the one to blame
In this life, none of my wishes even tried to come true
And the only special thing that I had was u
Now you're gone, and I'll have nothing to share with my kids
Not even memories to share about the things that we did
And I cry, every night I got a tear when you're gone
And I have nothin or no one to help me get thru the storm.

I guessed u used drugs ta keep ya head above water
But they made u forget u had three sons and some daughters
I know u sorry for the pain dat u caused,
taking advantage of the blessings dat wuz by God
but I forgive u and I know dat the Lord do
But my hardest pain is living in dis world without you.

Me, I thought dat we would be together not just a short time
If I knew I would've been a lil better.
I know I did take u for granted some times
Giving u lines
Telling you a million one lies
Making u cry
So much dat tears would fall from my eyes
But when u'd leave and come back man, things would get better
Now I cry all my days cuz u ain't coming home never.
Man, just to think of that kills my soul,
Just ta think about the world and it being so cold.
I just cry.

PART II: BUSINESS

Y'all are going to like this because it's about getting dat paper. In this section I deal with business in the hood. There's only one place you can get DVDs, CDs, G-Nikes, and an outfit with a matching watch out of the same place—and that's Orleans Avenue. We've got stores lined up from Rocheblave to Claiborne. We also have people in and around Lafitte like the frozen cup lady, bootleggers, and can collectors who make extra money at Southern Scrap.

We enjoy giving our money back to the community because no one else is. Most the store owners have been there since their children were babies and know 90% of the neighbors in the community. It's amazing how people can form a bond from meeting up in these places. We buy and talk because store owners want to know if you're fine and how's the family doing. People can't possibly understand the closeness of public housing until they've lived there.

DOOKY CHASE'S RESTAURANT: INTERVIEW WITH LEAH CHASE

Have you ever met someone who somehow just had an effect on your life by the power of conversation? I just did with Mrs. Chase, the owner of Dooky Chase's restaurant on Orleans Avenue. My teacher Ms. Rachel and I went to Dooky's to ask her if I could reprint an old interview for this book. I left Dooky's with the interview and a friend. Mrs. Chase and I talked for an hour about people. She believes that all people need to feel good about themselves is a little inspiration. She says that instead of ignoring the needy and stepping over the homeless we should help. Most people feel that as long as they're fine the world will keep revolving, but then there's people like Mrs. Chase. Some say that humanity died out a long time ago, but I think it could be reborn if we taught our children to love. Love is what we need in this world and Mrs. Chase helped me understand this more clearly.

BEGINNINGS

When I came up, I was the top of the line of eleven children and my place was never in the kitchen. My sister under me was in the kitchen. I would do what they called housework—you do the floors, you mop, you stay out of the kitchen!

In the black community we had many nice little spaces run by women. They were not big spaces. A lot of them were bars, but those women ran good bars, I'm talking no nonsense bars. They went to their bars dressed in their little uniform and they always wore this pretty handkerchief in their pocket , and they made money and they hired people. You don't have that anymore, but there were a lot of women in the black community that had little spaces, where they had maybe one table, or maybe it was a take out place. In the forties I used to go to one; that lady just had a little stove and a couple of little tables in there and she would cook the best butter beans I've ate in my life.

When I was eighteen years old, I went to work for a woman in the French Quarter. You know, usually they had waiters down there in the Quarter, but men were going to war so they had to hire young women. I went to work down there, and that woman taught

me a lot; she really taught me to love this business. I didn't know one earthly thing about a restaurant because it was segregation. There were no restaurants as we know them today for black people.

DOOKY CHASE'S RESTAURANT

This restaurant was started in 1939. It started as a little sandwich shop across the street, and then we moved on this side, but that was kind of like a new thing to the black community. I really liked it. I liked everything about food preparations. I've been in this kitchen for more than fifty years and there isn't one night that I don't take some food magazine or some something and look over it to learn from it a little bit more.

Cooking is something that you have to put a little bit of yourself in there. You have to learn what will blend with what, what will not overpower what, what herbs and spices [go with what] and that sort of thing. But you really have to enjoy food. You cook what you are. I came up cooking Creole. Creole is a mixture of things. You have Creoles everywhere. If you go to South America you are going to find Creoles out there; they are a mixture of Spanish and African. There are mixtures of people that would be considered Creole so you can't take a person and say, "Well they don't look like this so they aren't Creole." Or, "They don't look like me, so they aren't

Creole." If you go to Commander's Palace, for instance, [how] they serve Creole [is] totally different than what I serve here, because my Creole has more African influence, because that's my mixture.

FOOD AND COMMUNITY

You learn to cook a little bit from everybody. There's no better way to understand or learn about a person's culture than through their food. If you learn about their food, and take interest in whatever their food is, you will learn a lot about that person. You will come close to that person. Somedays we'll do Chinese things on the menu. We have one day that we do what we call, "wak and soul." You know, Chinese use wak pots so we do shrimp fried rice, sweet and sour chicken wings, or we may do peppered steak. On the other side of the buffet we'll have greens, sweet potatoes and pork chops.

I am now about to take some time out on Saturdays to visit the Vietnamese village out in the East—I have never been to their market—to see what they use. I love lemongrass in chicken soup. I like that, but there are other greens and other things that we could learn to use, and learn about these people. Lemongrass is a great restaurant and it's Vietnamese. That's new to us here, but I think if you learn about them, and learn about their food, that would help both sides. When people are coming, you can't alienate anybody; you can't do that. If they come in your community, you have to work with them and help them learn about our culture and make them see our way of life, but that doesn't mean they have to give up everything that is theirs.

Neighborhoods are what you make them. This business of leaving a neighborhood because this is happening or that is happening, I think that is— I can understand you leaving maybe if you want a bigger house and if you have more children you want more space—but people have to learn to start building their own neighborhoods. This restaurant has been here more than sixty years. Nobody ever touches anything here. My neighbors look out for me. I don't have a guard. I don't need a guard. My neighbors aren't going to let you or anybody else do anything here. They aren't going to do anything here and they aren't going to allow you to do it, because I treat everybody like human beings, and they are.

All of us have a job to do on earth and that's to make the world better. To make our space better and if you just don't look at the next person and help him do what he's supposed to do, then you're missing the boat. People need to build their own communities— build 'em back up.

OASIS UNI-SEX BARBER SHOP:
INTERVIEW WITH FREEMAN LOUIS

Freeman owns a barber shop on Orleans Avenue right across the street from my grandma's house. He inherited the business from his father. He says, "Basically this has been my home all my life." Freeman has an older crowd of customers who don't think of it as just a place to get a hair cut. They consider the time with their barber a time to relax. A lot of men often hang in front or inside of the shop laughing and drinking—just having a good time talking about the old days and how they miss them, how music ain't the same no more and kids these days have no respect. When I asked him for an interview, he was hesistant and explained, "I really think that there are older people out there who've experienced a whole lot more than [me]." When I told him that his perspective was important, he relented and said, "I am ingratiated with your company, as far as being looked at as interesting."

LAFITTE

The Lafitte Project is so centralized. It's so centralized that at some point everybody from Uptown that wants to go Downtown has to come through here. At some point everybody that comin from outta town and comin into town for work has to come through here. Feasibly, this area, consciously or unconsciously, is goin to play a role in your life.

It could have a garden theme or something that's more invitin for people that's more or less just passin through everyday. Just because it's the projects doesn't mean that it shouldn't have palm trees in the neutral ground. A lot of projects seem to be places that put out messages with madness [instead of recognizing all the] creative people [who live here] with very thoughtful skills. [Maybe these people] do not have the support, do not have the black power, do not have the spiritual inspiration to follow through on some of the ideas that's in their head to make this place a better place.

MOVING TO THE CITY

My grandparents moved from a country town which was called St. Francisville and the county is Point Lafitte. At that time, they had already gone through the Depression, and really to live like a sharecropper can be a very unstable situation at times. Some years you can have a bumper crop, other years you can have a bummer crop.

[In New Orleans my grandparents] perpetuated a fruit and wildlife business. They sold tomatoes and vegetables, but they also sold kale, rabbit, chicken, fish. It was what we considered country food. Wild-

life. They sold it right around the corner on Galvez between St. Ann and Dumaine streets. They had connections in the French Market with people that were transporting different fruit, vegetable, wildlife from these country towns. They tried to maintain a quality level of service along with a quality level of product along with a quality level of human being.

My grandmother on my mother's side had sixteen kids. On my father's side, they had seven. Basically we had our own social circle within our family. We had a strict family discipline type situation that made sure that everyone was more or less responsible for the one under them. In other words, if you were six years old, you were responsible for someone five years old. It was sort of like a step ladder type discipline.

So many moved [into the city] until they were able to buy this four-plex. [There] was enough room for everybody to live in that four-plex. It needed work done on it, but we had skilled laborers that were in our family. Basically, it was a situation of being between a rock and a hard place and making a house out of it.

LEARNING A TRADE

My mother was a beautician and my father was a barber. [This] shop's been open since 1952. My father was very much aware of the fact that at one time a man took on manly responsibilities. He went to work at maybe six in the morning to four in the evening. He used to go out and find guys that didn't have jobs but that wanted to work, and he would give them employment. Came here for maybe five in the evening to nine at night. He had a partner that worked along with him for about twenty years, so it was comfortable enough for him not to have to carry the whole burden.

I've been in the business since I was nearly out of high school. I started cutting here, with a license, about the age of seventeen. And now that I'm forty-seven, I guess I've been a participant in the business for at least thirty years. I'll tell you the truth. It's just like if you take a puppy and you keep em locked up until you think he's mature enough for you to let him roam. There's no guarantee that he's gonna come back home, but if you instill the proper values in your dog or your child or whatever, you can entrust them with being able to go out there and find a bone, and bring the bone back home and provide for the rest.

I traveled because I wanted to get different ideas of what was going on in different places. There was a lot of blacks that were spending a lot of money lookin good, but their hair was still fallin out—too many chemicals. Just because something's being sold doesn't necessarily mean that it's something for you. They're selling it to make a dollar. If you should opt to buy it, they're not necessarily obligated to tell you, "This wasn't formulated for you." For the past twenty years, there [have been] certain things that work meticulously to grow black hair, just like it works meticulously to grow white hair. It's just a matter of how much time you have to find people that are going to invest in a situation to benefit ethnic people.

OASIS UNI-SEX BARBER SHOP

All I can really do is provide a service and provide a value system. Sometimes you have people that participate in supporting their own, opposed to supporting other cultures. I [was] blessed enough to come up during the time when black cultures supported black cultures. I was once associated with the Muslims and I was able to be enlightened to the fact that spare change is no way to help a person to grow and to learn how to grow. You see, opposed to saying, "I'm gonna give you food stamps," I would prefer for you to teach me how to grow the food. [It's important to be] able to pass that on to someone else and make that universal.

Today, my customers are seventy-five percent male. Cultures evolve, but the basic thing is representing manly connotations. At one point, you know just what cut belongs on what man. I basically like neat, conservative looks. I'm not that thrilled about a man having too much hair. Before the bush, you had to take the down cut. Along came the perm. [Although] the perm has been here since the fifties, it just wasn't a natural thing for the average black male to conform to [when] you're going be out there throwin balls, or being around dust and dirt. Now, you go to the Afro, that's just too hard to do that. You may be trying to make a political statement, but as far that Superfly thing, that's supposed to be knockin everyone

The youth out there now want to be the same, but then they still want to be better than each other. They try to distinguish themselves and these ten-

dencies become fads. I try to keep them mindful that being conscious [of] hygiene as a whole gonna help [them] get down that avenue [they're] pursuing much quicker. This makes me think about something. There's a guy I need to see about a haircut that I gave him recently. I cut his hair twice— same cut. Both times he said it was getting better because I cut it. But then when he went around his peer group, and his peer group felt as though by him changing that he was more or less tryin to, in a subtle way, say that, "There are things I can do."

There has to be certain efforts that have to be designed to preserve the male, the man. They're dying at such a young age here. If the fathers that made them would contribute more time toward developing them, then we won't be lookin down the line at extinct creatures.

BUSY BEE CORNER STORE:
AN INTERVIEW WITH FADI ABU ALI

When you go in Busy Bee, you always get a good laugh because Mike and Ken are throwed off. Mike knew my whole family—my dad and all. Ken only worked at night, so I didn't see him much. Mike was always there when I went to school, came home from school, and even when I went to get my thrity cent juice on the weekends. He was always there cracking jokes saying, "What's up lil' mama" or "Holla at me when I get my FEMA check." Just anything to make you smile. I did an interview with Mike and learned that Mike isn't his real name afterall. . .

PALESTINE

My name is Fadi Abu Ali, but sometimes people call me Mike because it's easier for them to say. My birth date is April 11, 1963. I'm from Palestine, Jerusalem. They have three religions over there, which is Muslim, Jewish, and Catholic. Each religion has different churches, mosques, or temples where you go pray. The Muslims pray in a Friday. Jewish people, they be on Saturday, and Catholic or Protestant is going to be on Sunday. We have a lot of problems over there, but I pray every day for peace. You know, that's what we're lookin for. Some peace and a place to live.

We belong to Palestine. In 1948 Jewish people came from somewhere we don't know, with the British people, and start kickin the Palestinian Muslim people from them village, from them houses, and a lot of times they killed people, too. Oh, yeah, they shoot people and they take over. So they kick them out and Jewish people took over. We don't have no power to fight back. We don't have no guns. See, they got all the guns and tanks. Now, a lot of Palestinian people in 1948 ran away because they're going to die. Nobody like to die. So now they live in a camp, some of them have no roof. They have a lot of Palestinian people that live in Jordan, Lebanon, and Syria, which is not our country, but it's our people.

Now the kids, who was the babies in 1948, they're grown—forty, and fifty, and sixty—and now they fight back to get the land. [In] the last ten years a lot of Palestinian people die [in the *intifada*]. Why? They fight for their rights. When they fight for their land, the government call that terrorism. What I'm terrorist for? I'm fighting for my land. Somebody try to come with a gun over here, and try to rob me. I do the best, you know, to knock him out. But if he shoot, I have no choice. Same thing, they come over, they take the land. But it's hard because they got power. Your tax, my tax, going overseas to support them.

The point over there is [the Israeli government] want a land with no Palestinian people. They keep kicking people out. They always want to take, take, but they never give. If you want to go somewhere to go shopping, you have a checkpoint. You can't pass. You have to show your id. And they look at your ID and if they don't like you or maybe this picture don't look like you, and you be traveling like a couple of hours in a car, and they'll send you back home.

I remember when my brother went overseas in 1996. We have passports. American citizens. He went over there for vacation. He wasn't married so he went to the mosque at nighttime to pray. When he walk out, the Jewish soldiers be walkin the street with the guns. He asked him for an ID. They want a Palestinian ID. My brother, he carry the passport. He showed them the passport to the soldier. The soldier look at the US passport, dropped on the floor and stepped on it. And they kicked my brother butt cuz because there was nobody in the street. For nothing. The man comes to the mosque to pray and go home. And they catch him and get upset because, "How he get the passport?" They hate to see us American citizens.

You know, sometime we try to support the Palestinian people—the father or mother or uncle die and give them a few dollars, just to feed them and buy them clothes, and the government over here, they say this money is going to support terrorists. Ain't no terrorists. Why you callin me a terrorist? They're human beings, like us. We have to live.

USA

I used to work in concrete, sheetrock, all kinds. When I used to go to Jerusalem, I used to see American people because Jesus came from there and they want to go see what his life is about. It was my dream to come to USA. I think the USA is for fun, you know what I mean? You go to the USA and come back with the money, build houses, buy cars over there, so there must be like mountains of money. Just go over there with a paper bag, and start shoveling the money! That was my idea.

I came to USA in 1983. You know, my daddy was over a corner store and I start to help him. It's hard. Start going to the store from seven, come back home at seven. When I used to go to sleep, I used to cry at night. I say, "What the heck I'm doin here?" I didn't think I'd come over here and work like that. I see people workin twelve hours, fifteen hours. That's not life, you know. Step by step we start buying other stores.

MARRIAGE

I met Ms. Wafa in Chicago. When I came to USA, I worked for four years and I had a couple of dollars. I was twenty years old, so it was time for me to get married. My sister lives in Chicago, and she told me, you know, "Come over and we go visit. You might see each other, maybe you get married in the future." If I go to house by myself, I'm not welcome. You have to have family on my go to her house because she's only one person over there. So when I went over there. She was slim jim. She fine lookin. I told my sister, "Maybe she's the one, but maybe she don't like me, you know?"

Almost two months we keep going by her house, and they come by us, and then I mentioned to her parents, "I would like to get married to your daughter." Her father and mother say, "Well, we see what we can do for you." I left Chicago and came back Louisiana, and started back at the store I'm workin, and then a month later my sister called and said, "They agreed with you and everything's going to be okay."

I go visit them again. We sit with the family and start talking. You know, we want to get married, we have to talk—see how she look, the way she talk, and everything, to make sure of your choice. We start liking each other, but we cannot date because we have to get married. I buy a ring and stuff and after three months engagement, I went back to Chicago and get married.

CORNER STORES

I was working in this rough, rough store in the Florida Projects. Everyday, killings and shootings, you know what I mean? But life is just taking a chance. I think, "I have no choice. I have wife and children. I have to raise my children." But really, sometimes, I sit down and think, "What I'm doing in that area over there?" I have a lease in the Florida Project for like fifteen year, but I stayed just three and half and left. [I started thinking], "Hell with the money. Money comes, money goes, but if I go, who

will take care?" You know, we trust and everything, but it's hard for me working in tough area, and just leaving my wife and my kids at home and never know if I would come home.

After I sold the store in 1994, I went back [to Palestine]. It was different; new buildings and new people. All the people that be my age are traveling to support their families. For three months I stayed over and seem like I was gone for one hour and then it was time for me to pick up and come to USA. You know, we get upset because we leave our people behind to come over here, and we never know what's happen to us or what happened to them over there. But thank God we're livin, you know what I mean?

It's a money thing that makes us stay in the USA. You say "I'm gonna stay five years, make enough money, go back home and get married and stay over there." But when you make ten thousand, you decide, "I want to go make fifteen. I'm gonna make twenty." And then we get married and have children. The kids speak Arabic, but mostly they speak English, and they go to school. Our kids in USA school, they're very smart. They speak two languages. I have two girls and boy going to school and they get B sometime but mostly like they get A, A+. If they have a project, their mother might help them. That's why I keep my fifteen-year-old son away from the store, because I don't want him to be in a grocery store in the future. He can go to school, get an education, be a doctor, lawyer, electrician. You know, something much better than the father.

BUSY BEE

When we came back, Wafa was thinking I was coming back to sell the furniture and cars and we fly to Chicago. I like Chicago, but not the snow and cold. I have been here more than twenty years. It's okay with me. I started searching for a nice area that I could live with. I chose this here, because it's right on a main street, cars are in and out, police are in and out. I've been here a long time. I came to this corner in 1994.

You know, you have to be friends with people. Where I came from, I wasn't a rich man, so I feel for the other peoples, so I look out for them. I really don't have no problem, but sometimes you have to watch who you're dealing with, you know? Some people, you look out for them and they make it habit. They come back again, "Can I have this? Can I have this?" Sometimes we give them credit, and they stop coming this way. Sometimes I catch them, and I say, "So what happened? Where's my money?" "Oh, I don't owe you no money—you got your people mixed up." That's anywhere you go: you have to watch your back.

Since I got married and have children, I feel for other children like I feel for my children. Sometimes they come to me at 8:35, and I can't bring them to the store, because they have to go to school. I say,

"Look, I'm sorry." They say, "Please, can I have a bag of chips?" So sometimes I sneak them some stuff.

On Halloween night, believe me, a lot of stores shut down early to run away, because they want to give no candy to the kids. And the mother of the family always spend money, so it's time for us to support them. What I do is go to the candy place, buy me like forty, fifty dollars of candy, and when they come line up at the door, each one gets something in the bag. A lot of stores shut early because they don't want to give some away. They think it's scary. It's not scary, it's that they're too tight.

My people, my people! The thing is respect and love. I don't say that just to make money—no. You have to be friends. You have to respect each other. It doesn't matter what color we is, we are all human beings.

FROZEN CUPS

The best frozen cups in the world are sold in Lafitte for only twenty-five cents. You get the flavor of your choice: strawberry, grape, orange or any of the others. When I was young, my friends and I would do anything to get a quarter—including selling cans at Southern Scrap, helping people with their bags, cleaning yards—anything to get that frozen cup. Man, they were good.

DVD'S AND CD'S

Manufacturers say bootleggers are crooks. We say manufacturers are the real crooks selling CDs for $19.99 and higher when if you own a computer you can get them for free. See, they know this and they also know that poor people can't afford computers, so they take advantage of that. In my opinion, that's crooked. On Orleans Avenue you can find anything you want: movies, music, clothes and shoes and it won't send you to the poor house. When you buy from bootleggers, the money stays in the community and that's what we need—more money in the community. Bootleggers also offer quality product and if it doesn't work then you get a full refund— unlike stores with the NO REFUND sign as soon as you hit the door. I just prefer to buy from people I know as opposed to big stores that don't know me.

SOUTHERN SCRAP

In most housing projects and other neighborhoods around the city, churches or community centers supply poor or low-income families with food, clothing, and other resources they can't afford. In the Lafitte, we have also have another source: Southern Scrap. You would never in a billion years think that this place helps homeless people, but it does. See, Southern Scrap is a recycling company. They buy cans, copper, and other material you can find on the streets.

Many homeless people as well as some residents of Lafitte look for cans, old parts, or anything else they can to sell to Southern Scrap for some money to make it through the night. And the next day they're back at it again. It's sad to witness. People dig in dumpsters to get a few cans or scraps of metal but like this homeless woman Teedy used to say, "Y'all don't understand, I gotta eat, too." But you know what? I do understand. These people depend on Southern Scrap to live and survive. Other people in my neighborhood understand as well because they leave cans and other things that they're eventually going to throw away on the ground so that can collectors can pick them up.

Grandma Pearl was a very big help to a bunch of the can collectors. I remember many a night having to go drop cans on the side of the porch for a woman she knew. Every night she would stop by to get her cans, say thanks, and then keep moving. She used to tell us kids, "You can't make money in one spot, baby. You gotta keep pushing. You gotta keep moving."

HANO started a policy, which stated that no trash can be left outside or you will be evicted. My grandmother and other residents of Lafitte stopped leaving cans outside. My grandmother wanted to help, but she didn't want to lose her house either. Some people still leave cans in their house and when they see their "regulars," they'll give them a bag they've saved.

BURIED IN THE PROJECTS: THE STORY OF SOUTHERN SCRAP AND THE HISTORIC LANDMARK COMMISSION

When I first met Mr. Clyde he ran my teacher, Ms. Rachel, and me off Southern Scrap's property. But before we left, we gave him a story I had written about the scrap yard and told him to call us because we wanted to do an interview for this book. He kept the story but didn't seem too into it.

Weeks passed. One day on my way home, a truck came down the street. It looked as if it would hit me, so I jumped the curb and the truck stopped. It was Clyde. He told me he'd been looking for me for weeks but couldn't track me. He told me that Southern Scrap would be declared an historic landmark. At first I thought it was great, but soon learned it really wasn't. See, the scrap yard would then need to be repaired, and Southern Scrap was concerned that, "it would have potentially raised the cost of doing business without a real benefit to the neighborhood." If Southern Scrap closed, a lot of the customers who depend on the yard wouldn't be able to sell their scrap and make money. That's where I fell in. He needed me to submit my story of Southern Scrap to the historic landmark board. Ms. Rachel and I talked, and we decided to go. When we arrived at the Historic Landmark Commission meeting, Mr. Clyde along with some scrap yard customers, were standing outside. That's how I met Ms. Dorothy. She's a short black lady with all the kindness in the world.

At the meeting, the Landmark Commission brought up the "old art deco building that was buried in the projects." But after Southern Scrap's lawyer explained the importance of the building as a scrap yard, the board realized that while they were trying to help preserve the building, in this case the designation would cause more harm than good. We all took pictures after the meeting and Mr. Clyde and Ms. Dorothy agreed to be interviewed for my book. Southern Scrap is still open and running and Ms. Rachel and I have gained new friends.

INTERVIEW WITH CLYDE SMITH

Ashley: Where were you born?

Clyde: Cheneyville, Louisiana

A: What was it like out there?

C: It was a country town. A lot of farming cotton and sugar cane. Really, it was a historic community. You have a lot antebellum homes in that area. I grew up on a farm. My parents had five of us. I picked cotton and potatoes.. I pulled corn. I did it all. I was brought up the right way. Sunday school on Sunday mornings. A good Christian life.

We moved off the farm when I was about ten years old. The large farmers [were] going around buying up the small farmers. It got so bad until they couldn't make any money off of it. They gave up the farm and my daddy became a janitor at a school and my mom worked in the hospital as a cook. My daddy saved enough money from selling the farm to buy a house. We lived comfortable, you know.

You know, they don't regret it [but] I miss some of it because I'm still trying to plant a garden. There's nothing like your own fresh vegetables. Daddy still plants greens and tomatoes and stuff like that. But they're old right now. My parents are 84 years old. Both of them are in good health, so I thank God for that.

I lived in Cheneyville for eighteen years, then I went off to trade school. I took a trade in welding, and I worked in Shreveport for two years. The company I was working for went out of business and I decided to come to New Orleans.

A: How did you?

C: Well, I got up one morning and told my mother I was going to New Orleans. I had twenty dollars in my pocket, a loaf of bread and clothes on the back seat. That's how I came here.

A: What did you do when you got here?

C: I got me a map and I started riding around the city. I asked a guy over on the Industrial Canal where I could find a job and he told me to go to Southern Scrap. I went to Southern Scrap and got hired.

A: The same day?

C: The same day.

A: That's good. How long have you been working at Southern Scrap?

C: Thirty-six years. I ran the trucking department [before I was transferred here a few years ago.] When I came here I saw some things I never seen before. You know, with people pushing baskets.

A: Do you think it's a good way to make money selling cans?

C: Most people from here don't have another income. There are so many people who really want to work, but they don't have the work for them to get. There's no work for them in the city. [One of] the problems we have in the city [is that many] people have some type of arrest record. When you go for an interview for a job, people look at your record and they won't hire you. There is no rehabilitation for these people when they get out of jail.

A: What kind of people come to the scrap yard?

C: Well we have homeless people, unemployed. The first thing most people want when they come here is a job from Southern Scrap. I try to know their name. If I haven't seem them in a couple of days I'll ask, "Where have you been?" I have developed a pretty good relationship with most of them on a business level.

A: I just really, really liked it when I was young. I mean, we used to walk around the project with a big basket and we used to pick up cans just so we could get some money to get some food. Do you think it's helpful?

C: That's a good question. If there were jobs for these people—

A: This is like a tourist attraction, New Orleans.

C: Yeah, that's all we have is tourist stuff.

A: In other places you have other jobs.

C: And that's right. And really the main problem is the school system. You have to start with educational side of it first. And they're not doing that here. Orleans Parish School System is the bottom. You know, until that changes, we're still going to have this problem with people not getting good jobs because the educational level is so bad. But people here taught me a lot. I learn a lot from them. They taught the good from the bad. You know how to handle people—give them respect and you'll get respect back. That's what I try to do with most of them that come here. I don't care how they look or what they have—I treat everybody the same.

INTERVIEW WITH DOROTHY GRACE

Ashley: Where were you born?

Dorothy: I was born in Pineville, Louisiana. North Louisiana.

A: What made you come here? Why did you come here?

D: Well, I came here in the early seventies and I was going to school. I went to Booker T. Washington. I quit school in eleventh grade. That was a mistake. But I started pushing the basket. I do that because it's freedom to walk around and meet people and be outside. Freedom of not being cooped up.

A: Do you live in Lafitte?

D: No, I don't live in Lafitte. I live on Claiborne by the Circle Food Store. I enjoy doin it. I get up every morning. I keep my same basket and I just go walk around and hustle.

A: You know a lot of people that come to this place. Do you think this is a real good way for people to come and make money?

D: Yes, it is. You don't steal. You don't turn no tricks. You just get up, get a basket, and get out there and get it.

A: You're your own boss.

D: You're your own boss. That's all right and you don't have no set hours.

A: And do you have like friends that...

D: I have a lot of friends that do this. If they don't sell it this day, they'll sell it tomorrow. You know, but they get up and make an honest living.

A: And it really is an honest livin.

D: All over this city you walk around

Rachel: What are some of your favorite places to find cans?

D: I walk Elysian Fields to Esplanade.

A: What would you say to the people who judge you?

D: Well, that she's a good honest woman that choose not to do wrong to make money. But I don't meet mens out there. I stay away from them kind of people. I have people who give me clothes, shoes, and all kinds of stuff. If I can't use it, I'll share it with somebody who can.

A: If you could get another job, would you get another job?

D: Well, I worked when I was able to work, but I can't any more. I look forward to getting up and going to work with my basket. [laughing]

A: People who can work but don't have jobs at the time, do you think the city helps with that at all?

D: Well, if they would put out more work for the people, yes, they would. There's a lot of people going to work. They're not lazy. They don't want to steal.

R: Do you have any other family members in New Orleans?

D: I have one sister across the River. And I have a daughter who lives across the River.

R: You have a route of people who save their cans for you?

D: Every week, the same people save em for me, and I pick em up from their house. When I don't have them, I just pick them up from the side on the street. I pick up my little scraps and bring them and I'm early bird.

I come here every morning and I ask Mr. Clyde for a cup of coffee. I love coffee. I look forward to comin and my havin my own thing all the time to sell— not somebody's else's. I don't touch nobody else's

things. Sometimes people are so nice. They drop stuff off and if I'm out there or one of us out there, we get it.

I haven't had any problems— thank the Lord. I don't get in no dispute with no one. Never have. I don't sit around and get drunk and all that. Yeah, I'll drink a beer, but I'll go outside the yard over across the street. I don't over-indulge. I make an effort like a regular job and enjoy it.

A: I work and I hate my job. I hate my job.

D: So what's the name of your job?

A: I'm a cashier at a barbeque restaurant.

D: Well, I hope you move up one day. I hope you have a great promotion.

53

PART III: VIOLENCE

Respect is something that most people want. If you have respect, you have power and power always feels good. People earn respect in different ways. Some just respect you and hope you respect them back. Others run in yo house, put the heater in yo mouth and blow your light clean out to get it. Respect can cost you your life because if you tell people things they don't like, they make think you're disrespecting them and they'll kill you. Yes, kill you.

People I know who sell say, "They just making a living cuz it's hard." But, it's more than that, too. Once I asked my uncle, "Why do people deal drugs?" He told me "Respect and power. They might say it's to make a living, but it's respect and power. Once you get it, you feel like a leader."

I see movies nowadays that only show rich people with connections getting the respect and power. The life of a drug dealer, in particular, is made out to be glamorous. They get all the girls, the money, and the power and respect. It's not a good image for young kids because that's only half of the story. They should show the shoot-outs, the pain, the in and out of jail, and the death— it ends mainly in death.

POPPEE – TRUE O.G. (ORIGINAL GANGSTA)

Poppee is what we call a veteran of the game—one who has put in a lot of work and gets nothing but respect when he comes through, cuz young and older catz know how he's coming. It's like he's the Godfather of the Lafitte. Everyone knows him—not just people in Lafitte but other places. Poppee is very, very street smart. He's got the game down packed. Girls jack his style and younger guys hate to hear his name, but dats their problem cuz just like in dat movie State Property, "It's either get down or lay down." I'm just gone leave it at that.

He's intelligent. I learned that by interviewing him. Poppee understands something people spend forever trying to find the meaning of, and that's life. He understands what doesn't kill ya makes ya stronger. He had a hard life: mom passed at eleven, father not handling up. But he's a survivor. Bad things happen, you just gotta move on. Every hood has a legend. Ours is Poppee.

INTRODUCTION

I've always been the leader. You know, I never was a follower and I pride myself on that. My mom used to tell it to me, "You gonna be a leader cuz you always outspoken." With leadin come wisdom, and I got a lot of wisdom from growing up in Lafitte. The older people, they could see the wisdom in me and they just gave me the name Poppee because the name basically sound like an old man name. Poppee. You know what I'm saying? And that's why they gave it to me. You know how you can see how a person is going to survive in jail? Well, the old timers used to tell me, "See, you, you gonna make it if you go to penitentiary." "See that dude, Poppee, he can make it cuz he can think."

I had to survive from young. My mama died when I was eleven. She used to drink a lot and she had ulcers in her liver. She was bleeding on the inside and she just didn't want to go to the hospital. It killed her in her sleep. Before then, the only thing I could do the wrong way was to steal bikes. Everything else had to be done the right way— going to school, being respectful. Even today, I don't disrespect my elders. They might not like everything I do and the life that I've lived, but they never say that I cursed them to their face or raised my voice.

DEALING DRUGS

When my mom died, my fathers to my brothers to stepbrothers—all of em— were on drugs. My old-est brother was on the lease of the apartment we was livin in. After five or six months passed, he couldn't pay the rent. All of our furniture ended up getting put on the sidewalk and we got put out of the project. I started leaning on my lil' frinds, leanin on some of my kin people. I'll sleep a couple of nights here and a couple of nights there. Basically I just went from pillar to post.

When I was twelve, I got into selling drugs to get my clothes for school. My stepfather, who was married to my mom when she died, owned five or six houses. He saw that I was still going to school everyday and he didn't want me selling drugs. He was like, "I'm going to do what I got to do for you and I'm going to give you this house on St. Ann." That's right around the corner from the projects. I stayed round there. He said, "I'm gonna give you this house. I'm gonna pay all the bills for the house. Buy your school clothes and everything that you need— just finish school."

My stepfather was doin everything; I had my own house. I didn't have to do nothing but go to school. I made my first child when I was fifteen. I had my baby's mama stayin with me. She was fourteen when she got pregnant. Her mom was druggin, too, so she didn't care that she was staying with somebody else at that age.

I was supposed to do right. I had the opportunity

there to do right, but I was in denial. You couldn't tell me that drugs weren't the thing to do; you couldn't tell me I was doing wrong by sellin drugs. I didn't see the bigger picture—that if one person is smoking then really that hurts his whole family cuz his mother wondering where he's at or he's stealin from them. I went through this in my own family and still was in denial. I was the one in the family, as far as the brothers, that didn't use drugs. I just knew that from seeing them I wasn't never gonna go that route by using drugs. I thought that sellin was better.

MORNING AND EVENING DRUGS

You got your morning drugs and you got your evening drugs, you know what I'm saying? If you see a person up selling drugs early in the morning—six o'clock, seven o'clock—they sellin heroin. That's an early morning drug. It's a junk that people can't deal if they don't have it; they got to have it. That's the most addictive drug there is: heroin. Crack is addictive, but heroin is like a punisher. Your body gets sore, your bones get sore, you throw up. With crack, you're just tweeky. If you don't have it, you're just going to constantly fiend to have it. But heroin, you go into convulsions if you can't get it. You have people who work honest jobs that do heroin, so you got to get up early in the morning. You got to make sure these people can get their medication so they can go through their day.

Drugs are done all over the world. I drink and that's considered a drug, but that's as far as it go for me. Then you got some people who say, "I smoke weed and that's as far as it go for me." One can't down the other one. I just pride myself on not being on one

of the ones that have me stealing from my people or out here all night with no shirt on my back or willing to sell the shirt or shoes off my feet. You've got people who had prominent careers, who were set for life, and blew it because of crack cocaine. Heroin is the worst drug to be on as far as the addiction, but crack cocaine is the worst drug on as far as your morals. One thing about a person on heroin, ninety percent always want to be clean. They always looking at theyself, scratching and dusting themselves off. That's some of the reactions you get from a heroin user. But crack users just don't have no morals. They lose it. They steal from their mama while their mama's on her deathbed. Crack addiction is ridiculous.

CAUGHT UP IN THE HOOD

Once you're caught up in the hood, it's hard to get out, man. Because there's so much enjoyment and so much fun, you know what I'm saying? And you're not paying attention. You're young, and your life is not focused on serious things and responsibility. Your focus is on fun.

During the day, we'd hang in the driveway of the Wild Side. Laughin, jokin, bullshittin, runnin stuff. One of our partners might walk through, he just come home from jail so we talking about what he done when he was jail; start playin a little cards a little dominoes. At the same time, drug sales come through. We stop playing cards to make the drug sales. The females in the projects, they're surrounding us because they know we're makin money. They're laughin and jokin and playin with us. You know, we try to talk about hittin them that night. It becomes an every day routine. Later on that night, we might stop by a daquiri shop. Go out to club.

This is New Orleans. You can go anywhere at four, five o'clock in the morning. Barrooms still open, selling drinks. You're under-aged, you can still buy drinks—they don't care. You can go buy cigarettes, weed, anything.

Basically, I was just out there. I was just wilding. I didn't take heed to what my stepfather wanted to do; I was still staying in the house and he still knew I was selling drugs. It didn't matter to me. I was just doin what I wanted to do. I didn't take a heed to things 'til after I done 8.5 years between two times in jail.

THE STORY OF BLACK MOUTH

Let me tell you, this is a story that going to be with me for the rest of my life because it's like I was young. I had to be fourteen or fifteen years old when I witness my first murder. There was a guy named Kevin. His nickname was Black Mouth. He was cutting hair in the backyard, and I came round because I didn't feel like bringin my old lady and his old lady to work. Usually, I'd bring em or he'd bring em. We laughin about it, makin jokes while both of them standing on the side of us, trying to see which one of us was going to make the decision to bring em to work.

I was facing him. Comin from his backside, I saw a young dude running toward him with a gun in his hand. He was comin in our direction, but I didn't think that he was comin for either one of us, because you know, when the police went through the projects, people just break everyday with guns. [They] start running, trying to get away from the police, and really that's what I thought was happening.

Before I knew what was goin on, he had just stopped right behind Black Mouth, shot him in the head, and Black Mouth just like dropped in front of me. Blood was skeeting out his head up in the air, and he was just laying in front of me. The only thing that was separating me and the guy with the gun was Black Mouth on the ground. And the guy had put the gun back down to his side, but he was still lookin at me. And I was young, so I was shook up, but I knew not to run, because, you know, people react on fear when they're in that lifestyle. I just really stood there looking at him face to face thinking if he try to lift the gun up from his side, I'll probably have to wrestle with him for the gun.

It seems like a long time when I'm telling the story, but this happened all in a matter of ten, fifteen seconds. After the eye-to-eye contact, the guy turned and ran the way that he came from in the beginning.

Three weeks later, I was arrested on another murder charge. I went to jail and the DA came to me, because I was young, thinking that if they tell me if I rat on the person who murdered Black Mouth, then they can give me some leeway on the murder charge I was on. But I wasn't raised like that. In my hood, you can't be no rat, and that wasn't in me anyway, it just ain't feel right. They figured with me being young, the pressure would break me. They came and got me on the dude's trial date, put me in the courtroom, put me on the stand, and they showed me the dude. They pointed him out and then they asked me, "Do you see the person who murdered Black Mouth in the courtroom?"

I was like, "No, I don't see him."

The DA jumped up and say, "So you're telling me

this man sittin here, next to his lawyer—the state appointed lawyer sittin right there—is not the man you saw shoot Black Mouth?"

"No, that's not him."

I was the only witness. They threw the charge out. [We both] went back on the docks—you know, that's the place they hold you, before you go to court and after, to take you back to jail. He came to walk up to me to give me dap, like to thank me, cuz basically I spared his life as far as being incarcerated. He handed me his hand and I didn't reach my hand back. I was like, "Man, that was my little partner you killed. I didn't do you a favor. The way I feel about it, I want to get yours on the streets the same way you gave it on the streets. You know what I'm saying? I don't want to see you in jail. I want to see you dead, because you killed my partner." And we left it at that. He got out of jail and two weeks later I heard he was dead.

THE RULES WE LIVE BY

We don't have like gangs down here; we've just got like, "This is my lil partner. We from the hood. We grew up together; we cool." But it's not like we cool just cuz you from my hood—no, if I feel you jive or you ain't real, I don't want you in my company.

I could feel the way my lil friends handled themselves around me. If we had to kill somebody, and I get busted, I know I'm not going to rat and tell that you was with me. You know what I'm saying? And I can tell from the way certain ones handle theyself on the street—at least I can feel it, you have to go on your instinct—that he wouldn't do it for me. And some are just weak. And I know, I can't do nothing

with you. You can't live the life I'm living—if you get busted, you gonna sell me out. I ain't mad atcha, I ain't got no beef with ya, but we deal with each other on different levels. I might holler at you when we're at school, or whatever, but when we're in the street, I don't want you around me.

It all seemed fair game to me. It didn't seem like nobody was getting cheated. You know: "You weak, you beat. You strong, you move on." That's the rules we live by. We've got a thing, if you worry about something, that's when you get caught. If you think about the police catching you when you're going to steal a car, you get caught. If you worry about getting caught when you're going to jack somebody or shoot somebody, that's when you get caught. So repercussions don't even be on your mind. Second-guessing will get you caught up all the time.

[If your partner dies] and his lil birthday come around, you might throw a second line or dj, you know, to keep his lil memory going. But as far as me worrying about the other person involved coming back on me, it's self-explanatory. If you kill you somebody, they got people that might be lookin to kill you. That not nothing to worry about, though. I mean, they probably had some other people lookin to kill me before he got killed. It's intense on the outside looking in, but to me was a normal way of life.

BOXING AS FREEDOM

I was sentenced twenty-one years in jail for manslaughter. The murder took place when I was sixteen, and I had just turned seventeen when I got arrested. It was about four or five months later. It was a drug deal that went bad, that's all I'm going to say about it. It was a drug deal that went bad. The way I was raised up in the hood, you just don't let nobody take nothing from you.

After I was incarcerated for two years, my lawyer filed to have my sentence reduced cuz they said I was too young for such a steep sentence. The judge went along with it and reduced the sentence to seven years. At that time, there was a two-for-one law, which we don't have no more. I did three and half years on the seven and came home. Stayed home for like a year and one month and went back to jail on drug charges. They kicked the door in back here in the Tonti Court. They found marijuana, cocaine, crack cocaine, guns. I fought the charge for like two years and three months in jail; couldn't make bond because I was on parole.

I went to Angola when I first went up there. Then I was transferred to Angola to DCI and DCI to Wade. I was boxing while I was up there so we used to travel. As DCI boxing we'd go fight Angola one month, next month we go fight D'Quincy, next month we'll go WCI.

When you go to jail, you're trapped in a cell; you have no freedom. There ain't no sense in sitting around crying—judge has given you the time, you got to do it. Some people can deal with it, some people can't. I was one of the ones who were fortu-

nate to deal with it. Basically, the boxing thing was a way of freedom for me. Instead of being in a jail cell all my time, I'm thinking, "I could go fight at Angola. I've got some of my lil patnas that ain't never comin home. I go fight in Angola, I can go see them." You know, they'll be out there watching me fight. After I got off the ring, we'll probably sit down and kick it a little bit. You know, so it was a way of freedom. Instead of sitting in this one cell for five years, I got a chance at least once month to go outside, see freedom, get on the bus, ride the bus through the highways, and off the highways, and through certain towns. And that free your mind, that stops you from getting like what's called "institutionalized."

If don't have nobody doin for you on the outside— nobody to talk to on the phone, nobody writin you letters, sendin you pictures, keeping you in contact with what's goin on in the free world—sooner or later you loose your mental thoughts for the outside. You have people who come home from jail after being in there so long that can't adapt to freedom. They just have a one-track mind now. You know, once they locked up, they can't get out of that mode, and they call that "institutionalized."

OUTSIDE AGAIN

The five years that I was in there went to beating me up a little bit, touchin me up. Sleepin in there, you know, without being around your family. I went to thinking there are other things I could be doing. I came home with the frame of mind of working and things. I always thought that as I got older I would be lookin at other people who was working and what they was doing, because I wanted to learn that a little bit of that, too. I always did use my common sense with my street sense and I knew that this couldn't last forever. And so that what led to me dealing with the carpenter thing; learning from my father and a few other older guys that took time to teach me. I've had the opportunity to become a real good carpenter.

I know there's consequences to the life I've lived. Even though I've backed out of the game, I can't let my guards down. I know I done my dirt in the past, and I know what go around come around. The best that I can do is just be prepared for it.

I just try to talk to the youngsters and tell em about some of the stuff I've been through, you know. I can't make a decision for them but if they deal with it the wrong way, what the consequence is and if they deal with it the right way what's the benefits. You know, because I've been both ways and I've learned everything the hard way. If I can lend a helping hand, I'll help advice towards somebody—you know, I'll throw it—if they accept it or not, that's on them.

ANSWER ME

They told us to go school and our skills will enhance
Then they pushed us to the world where we didn't stand a chance
So they threw us some food stamps and told us we could spend em
Then locked us in the ghetto but we couldn't live up in it
And so we ride to earn the trust of the world
And so we ride, fire young boys and young girls
Cuz the future don't look too bright
Where is the light?
In the end one question, Will we be all right?

Dear Lord, answer my prayer, answer my prayer, answer me.
Dear Lord, answer my prayer, answer my prayer, answer me.

Who the hell are they to tell us we're not civilized
When they ridin in their Benz I know they hearin our cries
The cries of broken-hearted mothers who've been losin their sons
In the battle of life where you chose your own guns
It could be knowledge or rap or reload
When you're raised in the street, there's only one G-code.
"Do what you gotta do, survive the way you can"
Cuz they ain't got no room for a black woman or man.
And this world is based on one thing: the power of green
Having a life is a goal, but to us is a dream.
And I'm not tryin to blame them people for all my faults
But how the fuck are they gonna take water and give it a cost?
I'm sick of being here, livin under the dirt,
Seeing teardrops fall and I know it's the hurt.

Dear Lord, answer my prayer, answer my prayer, answer me.
Dear Lord, answer my prayer, answer my prayer, answer me.

Darrell

Cassandra

Head

Keitha

Kobe

Darnell

Charles

Tank

Kunta

Poochie

My cousin Jessie

Chucky

REST IN PEACE

Living in the hood you gain lots of friends. You also lose just as many. We honor our lost family and friends by getting their picture on a t-shirt. Some people go further to add a rag, socks, or a bandana. We wear them with pride when we second line down the street to celebrate their home-going. It's hard not to see people that you've grown up with. I've learned to stay strong and just wish them peace in the afterlife because once someone is gone, they're gone. I wish people who take and have taken life truly understood this—maybe one day it'll stop.

I've lost people through violence: friends, family or just people who lived in my hood. I try to remember them as often as I can, but my mind always wanders off because they are no longer here and I am still a part of this world. My thoughts always come back to them, though, because that's important: you're always supposed to remember so they can still live without being here.

WHY WE JUST STAY SILENT

I've learned a lot in my lifetime. Fifty percent of it was bullshit and fifty percent was real. The bullshit I got from grown-ups in my family who would rather lie about simple things like where babies come from than to tell the honest truth. And the real shit I got from friends and people I barely know who've seen and know a lot from experiences they've had. One of these people was Keisha. She used to be my friend but we've lost touch with each other. The realest shit I've ever learned from her is, "People killing and people being quiet is just the way it is."

I met my Keisha in eighth grade. We were fourteen-years-old and we attended Sophie B. Wright Middle School. I was living in the Methodist Home for Children at the time. I still remember how we met. I was sitting at a table in class by myself, wondering how it would be in a new school. Will I have friends or will people reject me for not having a functional family?

Keisha, who is no taller than Gary Coleman, light brown skinned and never on time for anything, came in late. Our science teacher, Ms. Johnson, used to say, "Keisha, girl, you gonna be late to your own funeral. Watch and see." There were no more seats anywhere except next to me. I honestly don't think that seat would've been her first choice. She sat down next to me and I am really glad she did. We ended up talking about the TV show "Friends," and I found out she loves it almost as much as I do. From that first conversation, we became close.

Keisha grew up in the St. Thomas Project, Uptown in New Orleans. She's seen a lot living there. I remember once she told me she saw a man get killed. She said she saw the killer and all. One night she was in the bed on the phone when she heard fussing. She went to the window to yell, "SHUT UP" but as soon as she got to the window she saw a man holding a gun and another being pushed to the ground. She said while she tried to duck down silently the gun went off and the man on the ground was dead. I told her about a similar experience. I saw a guy get gunned down on a back porch. My experience was horrible and frightening but Keisha spoke of hers as if it were normal. I once asked her why. She responded, "My mama says life isn't valued anymore and since they don't care about you, show no emotion for them. And if you see something, keep you mouth closed cuz it ain't your business."

It's funny how I understand this and also go by it. I only know because I've seen things happen that I can never understand—like someone getting sliced up because of who she is friends with. I have never talked about any of the things I saw. I think it's because I am afraid— afraid of dying and being alone.

Keisha says this makes me a coward because everyone dies. You were born alone so you shouldn't be afraid to die that way. Well, I accept being a coward, but I hate living in fear. Many people live that way in Lafitte. It's like you can't have anything without someone wanting it and willing to do anything to get it. People speak of days of sleeping outside on their porches, but I can't see that.

Keisha helped me understand why we stay silent when we know it's time to speak up. It's because we, as humans, are sheep. We need protection. Maybe not all, but most. And who is there to protect us? The cops? We stay silent and watch our friends' kids get killed; friends of ours get murdered. And the worst thing about it is we get stuck with all the memories that eat away at us. I know through personal experience, that's just the way it is.

WHAT GETS YOU PUT IN JAIL IN DA HOOD

In my project police set off an alarm of fear to the people who are supposed to be protected. It's like we're prisoners in our own community. I saw the police beat a boy once. I could've cried for him. The boy was a drug dealer everyone knew, including the police. One day they called him to the car. He took off running through the court. The cops chased him in the car. As they closed in on him, they hit him with the car—not hard, just enough to knock him down—and when they did, I think it was at least thirty minutes before they stopped kicking, punching, and spitting on him. I've seen some cops go so low as to mess around the minors. Although it can't always be proven, the truth is known. I just hope the force gets better over time and I thank God for the good cops who truly protect and serve.

#1. Being smart—and when I say being smart I don't mean smart ass either.

Example: You're walking down the street, police stops you and asks you for ID. You're spooked so you hurry and hand it to them. They run a check, you're clean. They tell you plain and simple, "Get the fuck outta here!" They even give you a push. You mumble a simple "Fuck!" You get beat, then go to jail.

#2. Hanging on your porch after dark

Example: One night you and your people got into it over something small. You go out to sit on the porch to free your mind. Two minutes into it, guess who rolls up? They wanna know why you're out. You don't wanna go back into that hole, so you say, "I am just minding my own business, officer." Ding, ding, ding: wrong answer. You get whooped, and then you go to jail.

#3. Watching someone else getting harassed and expressing sympathy

Example: You're on your way home from a hard day's work and you see the cops have some young guy on the car. They're slamming his head and back against the car. As you walk by, you utter, "That's fucked up how they doing that lil boy." Now you get a taste. They grab you, slam you. Now you're going to jail for interfering in police business.

INTERVIEW WITH UNCLE MICHELLE

My Uncle Michelle is forty-five years old, very tall light skinned and very, very slim. Most people who know him say he thinks he knows everything. The truth is he doesn't know everything, but he does know a whole lot. I love sitting on my front porch talking to him; he just makes things so understandable. We talk about all kinds of things: the world, the differences between the races—just life in all different areas.

My personal favorite topics to discuss are religion and issues in the neighborhood. My uncle is a Jehovah Witness and is always talking about how Christmas and Easter are just scams. He talks about which religion is wrong and how the end of the world will be. Sometimes I get a little spooked because I've read Revelations so I kinda have an idea on what it'll be like.

Me, I am not a believer in any type of religion. I am just a worshipper of God because I look at things in so many different ways that I can't just say, "Oh! I am a Methodist" or "I am Catholic," because I think that there is only one heaven and as long as we all serve the same God it doesn't really matter what religion we represent or if we even follow one.

My uncle didn't graduate from high school, but he does have his G.E.D. and a great job at Avondale Shipyards doing deskwork and some fieldwork. At a time in his life he did do drugs, but he never stole things and sold them. I guess he thought if he did something wrong he'd follow it up with something right so he worked to support his habit.

My uncle is very real. He speaks his mind and I love that about him. He tells it exactly how it is without cutting corners along the way. My uncle is the true image of a strong black man. He has survived so many downs in his life, yet he still has the ability to get back up and keep his head above water.

Maybe my uncle isn't a hundred-dollar-an-hour doctor or some fancy college graduate, but he is a man and no one can ever deny him that title because he earned it. He never gave up and I truly respect that. He makes me want to get up and do something just to say I did it.

Michelle: I'm forty-six years old, black Negro male, with no record, nothing. Everybody want to say, "Why don't you say it's black?" Know why? Because way back before they decided to say that you were black, you were colored. Then you were a nigger. Of course, I been goin to school and learnin with my education. There's two things I learned according to the King James version of the Bible: that everybody's human and that was it. Later you started getting race, you started getting color, wealth. I'm just human and I'm Negro. That's why when I fill applications and they ask about those, I don't even fill em out. Because I feel that is racist, not prejudiced, but racist.

I used to ride on the back of the bus. I used to get on the back of the bus with my ma. I just thought it was natural. I'll give you a great example. You heard of Master P? His little boy named Little Tokyo or something? Little Romeo. Okay. Here's a guy that his father came up in the projects, hard times and everything, taking an opportunity and left Louisiana and went to California and became a superstar. Has a son. His son don't know nothing about how hard things were. I seen an interview with him one time, and they asked, "Do you think you could live any other way than the way you do?" He said, "I could try, but it would be hard." Why? Because this is what he used to. That's the same thing. He's used to having whatever it is that he has because as he stated,

"I'm eleven years old and I've got fifty million dollars in the bank." Okay, now let's look at the guy who grew up in the project. The one whose parent had to scuffle and work, all right. This is what's natural to him. He has to work and strive. That's my answer to that. I know no other way, no other example, where a person can relate and understand.

I grew up in the Desire Housing Projects. I know what it is to be livin in the slums. I know when it's comfortable and I relax when I walk through here. I'm more relaxed when I walk through the Desire Housing Projects. But statistics say that's the two worst places there are. I'm like, "Really? Why?"

Ashley: What's it like being a black male livin in public housing?

M: What's it like being a black male? I have no idea.

A: African American— I mean Negro. I'm sorry, Negro.

M: Oh okay, what it's like being a Negro man living in the housing projects? There's no problem as long as you're friends with the police. Long as you are a friend of a drug dealer. Long as long as you're a...

A: Fifteen year old girl?

M: Well if you're a fifteen year old girl, you got it. But you said male. The people around here, in this area, refer to me as an undercover police. And I catch mayhem from the police. That's because I be by myself. I'm looking and I'm walking, cause that's what I'm used to, it's just natural.

I don't have a fear in this neighborhood. I'm from in this neighborhood. I know everybody in this neigh-borhood. Let me give you an illustration. If I came out of Lakeview, and came into the housing projects, the people that are referred to as criminals or thugs gonna realize that this is a new face. They are more likely to be assaulted than I am because I know the people. Not sayin that I can't be assaulted, but I would more likely to be killed because I can say who my perpetrator was. They more likely to be hurt, they would only be killed because of resistance.

Because I don't hang with what you call, I call em groups—society calls em gangs. I don't want to hang with a group of people or a gang. "I'm the law"—that's the mentality of individuals in the area. Like remember when we was walkin around and you had the little camera...

A: Yeah.

M: I told em, I said, "We doin this for the police"

A: Yeah. That wasn't funny. Not at all.

M: At all?

A: Not at all.

M: I know what they're doin. They fear, they're scared. I wouldn't care if you filmed me from now to Doomsday, I don't care.

THE POLICE AND SAFETY

I'm walkin down the street one day. Police came through and everybody scattered. I'm forty-six years old, Negro male, city of New Orleans, with no police convictions or anything, so I didn't move. They threw me on the car and totally harassed me. They ran checks on me from New Orleans all the way to Westwego. Then upon, when I got off the vehicle, he told me like this, "Get off my MF car." Because there was no warrant on me. They could not get me for trespassing. I looked at it, I even went through it. I said, "How many times you seen me in this neighborhood, and you'd ask me what I'm doing here. You know me." "No, I don't know you." It do you no good to try to argue. Don't do you no good to try to tell em something, because now you're setting yourself up for whatever charge they want to give you. The most prevalent charge in this is called "criminal trespassing."

You and I are sitting on the porch, they're subject to tell you, "You gotta leave." Even though you're my guest. And they will arrest you if you don't. And you will get that charge of criminal trespassing. It's not a good feeling. How do you feel when you go to the store and you buy something and you gotta pay eight percent tax on it? You don't feel good when the police are dictating to you.

One night, there was a guy that was riding a motorcycle and he had an accident. He was on a motorbike and he ran into a car. He went up into the air, and came down to it. They said he was dead upon impact upon the street. Police got there, before the ambulance. No one went over to try to see what they can do. They all waited for the ambulance. Police barricade everything off with their tape, and they got vulgar with everybody talking about, "Get back, get back." And you know the real reason why they did that, because they know this guy was a drug dealer. He didn't get respect because he was a known drug dealer. But he was a human citizen, he was still a person. He got killed that particular night.

They don't realize, "You are a law enforcer. You are not the law." They don't like to hear that around here. And I rub it in, if you bother me. If you don't bother me, I walk by. Because I wave at police. I won't run. Because I don't fear you. Because I'm not in violation of no law. Not in the Lafitte projects, you better do what you told. And the police tell you what to do.

A: Do you agree with the one-strike policy in the Lafitte?

M: Let's look at it. Let us define it as it is: one-strike policy. There's no room for error. That's a world of perfection. Who is perfect? I wanted perfect, perfection, I know about it in my life, Jesus Christ is the only one that was perfect. How can we get a one-strike? Everybody gonna make a mistake one time, everybody.

RELGION AND TRUTH

M : Well, let me tell you about this. This is my opinion of religion. I study under the Jehovah's Witness. One of the teachings is that Jesus Christ didn't come here talking about religion, he comin talking about his father's kingdom. He came to teach. Religion is something that people use to make money, okay. Under other denominations I have noticed that the pastor has a parking spot, the deacons have the parking spot, but the congregation is the one payin for everything. What makes these people special? They can't help you, they gotta die just like you.

People think that Jehovah's Witnesses are crazy. They're not, because they're imperfect people just like everybody else. We just try to lean more toward what Jesus' teachings were than other denominations and some people find it hard, because it's very hard tryin to follow those teachings. But as for other denominations, I believe in Jesus Christ as my Lord and Savior. And I believe everything he said. That's why I don't believe everything that I hear and see. Because if I can't research and find out by myself, it's a myth.

SNITCHING

In my neighborhood, people who talk too much get permanently silenced. It's just that real out here. People don't want their names mixed up in *nothing*. While doing interviews in Lafitte, I discovered this. I'd approach people with kindness and they'd be all for it until I tell them about release forms and show them the tape recorder. Then it was, "No, baby, I'm not bout ta get on no tape" or "I don't know nothing about back here." It didn't bother me, though. It inspired me to write this piece.

It's about how people are afraid to talk because they don't want to be labeled a snitch. But who would want to when the penalty is death? I've heard about people getting killed all the time for ratting. In my neighborhood, the worst story yet was this woman who was a local drug user. Somebody said she was ratting and it was over. The coroner stopped counting the bullets at forty-eight. Someone killed that woman. They took her life away all because someone thought she was trying to stop their hustle. It's sad. I wonder if it was true. I wonder if she was afraid.

RAIN, RAIN

Rain, rain, go away. Please come back another day, is all I thought about on rainy days in the hood. No one's outside, nothing's on TV and if there is, someone's already watching another show. I wonder where are all the usuals who hang in the project. You know, the hustlas, the users, the kids who see the transactions, the moms and dads, the homeless men and women who know nothing but the Lafitte. Where are they?

Once on a rainy day as this I realized something. Most people find peace on Sundays, "The Holy Day," but in the hood, we find peace on rainy days. Look out the window on one of these days and you'll see no one, and all you'll hear is raindrops. The kids playing, the women getting their hair fixed, boys playing basketball, and people making a living have all disappeared. There's just echoes of women shouting to their children, "Sit yo ass down," and guys hollering, "Come here, shorty. You fine, yeah."

See, Sundays come once a week but we all know rain comes every now and then so our peace isn't a weekly thing. It comes and goes, and to me, it's precious every time.

PART IV: REPRESENTING & CELEBRATING LAFITTE

People are never afraid to speak their mind in Lafitte. From freestyling to ward signs to official representation by the Lafitte Residential Council, we let people know where we're from and what we can do.

One of the things we're particularly good at is celebrating. We always have big events in Lafitte. From DJs to block parties to birthday parties to popping ass second lines, we put it down in the Sixth Ward. I think it says a lot when a a neighborhood parties together.

SIXTH WARD SIGN: 5+1=6

In the Lafitte and everywhere else in New Orleans we have hand gestures we use to represent our wards. The Lafitte is the Sixth Ward so we can put up three fingers on each hand. 3+3=6 or we'll put up my personal favorite: 5 fingers and a middle. I see it like, "This our ward, fuck u."

People in Lafitte respect these gestures because they let outsiders know where we live and how we coming. And believe me, we coming strong. At sec-ond lines we'll sing *Five finger and a middle flashed high in the air, Wild Side Lafitte where dem niggas don't care.* Not to start a fight but to let people know we in da house. Lots of people mistake our gestures for gang signs but they truly are not. They only remind us of how much we are proud of our hood. I know every time I put up 5 fingers and a middle it reminds me where exactly I came from and— for better or for worse—to love it.

GRAFFITI

ORLEANS & CLAIBORNE

Popcorn, candy apples, peanuts!!!!! Is all you can hear under da bridge on Fat Tuesday. It's like one big party where everyone is invited. Seventh Ward, Ninth Ward, any ward: people come together and enjoy being a part of New Orleans. We are all a part of what makes this city the big EZ. Great food and lots of fun and that is exactly what you get under the bridge. My first year of being under the bridge I had to be at least ten years old. I can't even describe the excitement in my eyes when we arrived. There were so many people all around. Grown ups, kids, old people, white people, black people, all waiting in awe to see the Zulu pass through. The kids were playing. Some were crying for candy apples while mothers are screaming, "We got food already!" Meanwhile, the old people dance to the jazz music that overflows the streets.

I was at the front of the parade crowd so I could see all the high school bands and floats. The people had black paint on their face with huge smiles, but I think they were smiling at all the people screaming, "Hey mister, throw me something." They all had beautiful beads they showed off to get the crowd more bucked up and hyped. The floats passed and we all were sad to see them go. Some kids were so broken hearted that they asked their parents to follow the floats all the way to Canal Street. After the parade passes, the party ain't over. Far from it. Daddies go straight to their BBQ pit and mothers set the plates while the grandparents and grandkids dance until it's time to eat.

BUT YOU SEE, PEOPLE DID A LOT OF MASKING BACK IN THOSE DAYS.

Claiborne! Everybody would go out early in the morning and go in the neutral ground—that's before you had the bridge. They had tables, they had barbeque pits and coolers from St. Bernard to Canal; it was a family thing. On Claiborne Street, that's where you saw most of the maskers: you saw the Indians, the skeletons, you saw the Zulu, and then some of the truck floats, which used to come that way, also. I was scared of the skeletons. Oh, I used to run from that crowd with the skeletons! The witch doctor. Ohh, I was running. I was afraid of that man. Also, my daddy and my *parrain* used to mask as women on Mardi Gras day. I remember one time, he had my mother's dress on and he came back in rags. They had beat the living daylights out of him. —Leah Green

MEETING ALL THE PEOPLE YOU HAVEN'T SEEN

The Zulu parade. The popcorn, the hot dogs, the beer. It's about everything: the Indians, the clothing, the laughter, the smiles from other people. Meeting all the people you haven't seen over the years. Faces. People come from all over the world to spend that Mardi Gras in New Orleans. It's just a beautiful thing.—Wanda DuBouse

81

"GET UP! INDIANS COMING!"

I come from over there on Conti and Tonti. We had the little shotgun house and my grandmother would wake us up at four o'clock in the morning and say, "Get up! Indians coming!" And I mean they would come! They would come from St. Louis Street. All the sudden you'd see the spyboy— the spyboy runs out there first, and he goes to make sure that nothing's coming—and then all of the sudden the spyboy dance. And they stood all the way around them and "My Spyboy!" and you'd see 'em. The neighbors would come running to em. And everything they did was handmade. They would be up all night right up to Mardi Gras. Yes indeed.

Other times, they would do their little practice and they would go to different barrooms and do their little singing and do their little dancing. I learned the dances by watching. And I think it's just in you. It's that soul.—Emelda Paul

IF IT'S IMPORTANT, YOU FORGET ABOUT THE COLD

Orleans and Claiborne. Mmm. That was back in the time. You know, I'm thinking about the bridge now, but it wasn't the bridge. It was just open. The little area under the bridge now was all trees from one end to the other. It's not cold now. It was that cold then. People would be bundled up with their coats, and their caps and gloves. But if it's important, you forget about the cold, and when the Indians came through, you were just gawkin.

Everybody's out there havin fun. You didn't worry about no fightin, no shootin in the crowd. They would cook and they would bring hot dogs, hamburgers, and chicken. Red beans, rice, smoked sausage, ham hocks, pickle chips and chocolate. Oh, it was good. Some people had a little get charcoal to keep the kids warm.— Annie Pearl Nelson

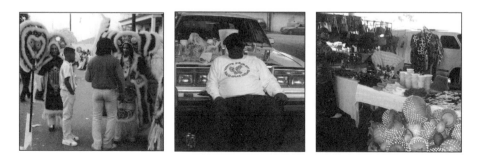

SUDAN SOCIAL CLUB'S ANNIVERSARY SECONDLINE PARADE, 2004

DOWN ORLEANS AVENUE

SUPER SUNDAY

People come from everywhere in New Orleans to see Super Sunday in the project. Sponsored by Tambourine and Fan, it's a parade for Mardi Gras Indians to show off their costumes. It begins at Bayou St. John and goes down Orleans Avenue to Claiborne. Old folks line up their chairs and young folks go snatch up their outfits, all to tear it down in dat Sixth Ward. We got music, Indians, and second liners who'll dance on top of your car if you don't stop them. We also have family—everywhere you look, you see family and friends. If it's mama and son, father and daughter, or two best friends just chillin, everybody's watchin the band pass. It's like Mardi Gras with more dancing than waving. Super Sunday is like the Sixth Ward's birthday. People come and celebrate how proud they are to be a part of a community like Lafitte. Some go home after the parade passes, and others follow the party to Hunter's Field on N. Claiborne and St. Bernard Avenue. And believe me, it ain't over until the sun comes up

FREESTYLING

A lot of people freestyle in my hood. It's a creative way of expressing yourself. People sit on porches, chill in the driveway—wherever the crowd is, you can bet they are freestyling and joking about how crazy what they said was.

In order to freestyle, you must first know how to rap. Rapping is a combination of writing and performance. Freestyling is more spontaneous. You say exactly how you feel off the top of your head. You can't write anything down.

In Lafitte people freestyle to nothing more than the ringer on their cell phone and it actually sounds tight. Domonique, Anthony, and I are always freestyling to ring tones just because it's fun and something to do. It helps you escape the life that bothers you and imagine a new one.

INTERVIEW WITH THE LAFITTE RESIDENTIAL COUNCIL

Four of my biggest fans are four very important women in Lafitte. They're a part of the Lafitte Residential Council. Their job is to make sure HANO is taking care of the tenants properly by making sure things work and the Avenue, the courts, and the driveways are always clean. But of all of the things they do, we in Lafitte know them the most for being the voice of our neighborhood. They hold meetings just to see if the residents are comfortable or have any suggestions. They also hold homework, computer, and adult literacy classes at the Sojourner Truth Community Center on Lafitte Street. They built the center with a lot of hard work.

I remember when they didn't even have an office, they were serving the kids breakfast and helping them out with their homework out of an apartment on Galvez. They were happy to let me interview them. They said it was great to see someone in the projects do something like write a book. I enjoyed talking to them and they had plenty of stories to tell about the struggle to get the community center off the ground. Ms. Paul also gave me photographs of her sister masking as an Indian on Orleans Avenue that can be found on the pages dedicated to Mardi Gras.

LEAH GREEN, FORMER PRESIDENT OF THE RESIDENTIAL COUNCIL

Since I was five years old, I've been living at 665 N. Derbigny in Lafitte. The resident's council was established in the 1970's. It started off with a number of committed activists, including Ms. Doris Sears, Ms. Leah Poree, Mr. Melvin Smith, and Mrs. Ursula. There were a lot of problems with the residents and something needed to be done. They got together and started going to the residents to hear about the problems they had. One of the reps would go to the housing authority and HANO would look into it. Other developments found out how that worked out with Lafitte; they started to organize, too.

Lafitte was the first resident council [in New Orleans]. After they started growing and years passing by, they had elections once per year for president. We would put fliers out for whoever was interested

in being on the board [and] working in the development. You have to do voluntary service for two years before you get on the board. A lot of people helped.

The rule was you have to be unemployed. You couldn't be working and be on the board. This is just like a job, but we're not getting paid for it. We all just volunteer our time. Even at nighttime, somebody may call my house or come by: somebody got water in their house, they claim they don't know the hotline number. I'll meet them out there and if something goes on, I can call the HANO hotline.

RESISTANCE

HANO always believed that the residents shouldn't have no say so. The residents shouldn't have governance over anything. But we thought different, you understand. Without the residents, HANO wouldn't have a job. We had residents that were a part of the Commissioners Board. They sit up on the board with HANO. HANO didn't like that because we had the say-so. We had one girl who would go to Washington, D.C. and guess what? HUD is coming down to see what the problem is. And if they're not satisfied with the way they was treating us, they let them know right then and there. They tried all kind of ways to break the resident councils up. But they see that they can't do this, because we govern them.

Citywide is composed of 12 public housing sites, in which each one of the residential council presidents sit up on that board. The citywide meets monthly. We would go to the meetings and get information to bring to the residents to let them know what's going on. Then we would travel to different workshops and meet with other residents in Washington, Frisco, wherever. New Orleans was the first board of com-

> *We're glad that you all are doing this because we want to tell the stories.*
> *If we don't tell the story, how the kids going to know what went on?*

missioners that had residents on it. They didn't have that anywhere else. When we brought our ideas to the others in public housing all over, then they tried to form their own. We also organized a statewide board, but that didn't last too long.

SOJOURNER TRUTH
COMMUNITY CENTER

We were working from 709 N. Galvez in an apartment and had been asking for years and years to get a community center. There were seven board members—all ladies. As soon as Mark [Morial] became mayor, we went to him and said, "Mark, it's like this. We want to get a community center. We have different programs but we have no space." He said, "Find out what place you want to go." We said, "We have the place already." This land here was for the railroad department. He said, "It's like yesterday you should have had it." He told us where to go to and [we] went right to the man with the railroad in City Hall. [That man] looked at the contract and said yes. Mark came back with us and we met again. [The railroad man said] he'll give it to us for one dollar for ninety-nine years. So this land's for us. We met with HANO and the city. We all sat down at the table and we talked about what we wanted, and it was approved. We got the architect and he came in to build the building. First, HUD gave us the approval; they had the money. This is still HANO's

buildings, but they have to come to us for certain things.

We went through a whole lot. We were supposed to be involved, but some HANO employees and contractors were having little secret meetings. When we came in to do a little walkthrough, there were things being done that we didn't know anything about. We wasn't pleased with what they was doing— and I'm not afraid to say it – we shut the door on them. We put a padlock on the gate—workers and nobody could get in. We sat outside and guaranteed they did not come in here because we wouldn't let them. Seven ladies got this together. Board members.

Michael Kelly finally came down when we threatened to get the news media involved. He looked in and he said, "I'm trying to do everything I could. What do you want?" We said, We want everything done right like it was supposed to."

I think one of the reasons we named it Sojourner Truth. She was on a journey. She believed in God and she talked and had faith in God. And she believed in the truth. Sojourner Truth. A strong woman. So you got a strong seven women!

EMELDA PAUL, PRESIDENT OF THE RESIDENTIAL COUNCIL

I lived right over there on Conti and Tonti—2403 Conti Street. I remember when this project was built. Back in them days it was nothing but houses over here. And then, it was the veteran area and the only people that lived in here was people that was in the service. And there were gray buildings and it extended from Prieur to Galvez and then from Galvez to Rocheblave. It was like low row houses; there was upstairs and downstairs.

On the weekends, they would have what they call a free show. They put a screen in the back of the office and we would sit on the fence. They would only charge us 15 cents to get over here Remember the skating? You know Union skates we used to get for Christmas? We used to take those skates, put them on 2x4s, and build up the skates. They would block Prieur Street off and we would have a skating party and pop the whip. At a certain time of night all you could hear was parents calling their children. My grandmother would get out there or would send one of us to call.

Back in those days, the people were very close, and not just anyone could get in this development. They had a hard time trying to get in here. You were screened, and the people took pride in what they were doing and how they lived here.

When I retired from Steamship International in 1994, I had a little time on hand. Someone said, "Well, Ms. Paul can help out." Mr. Harvey came over one day and asked me if I would be a block captain. I said, "Okay, what do I have to do to become block captain?" And he said, "Just find out the needs of the people in your area. When you find out what the needs are, then you can bring it to me and I'll bring it to the board." To get back on the board, I did a lot of volunteer service. When we had the neighborhood watch, I went all around me and then eventually, I was asked to be a part of the resident council.

GETTING INVOLVED IN THE COMMUNITY

The purpose of being on the resident council is not about me, but how we serve the residents in the community. Our children are our future, so therefore I work with the kids. I also work with the seniors. I remember Ms. Virginia's boys—God rest her soul—would get paint buckets, and they would play their little drums. There was about 15 of them, and you know, one of them was Trombone Shorty! Ms. Virginia'd say, "We got to get those children to stop playing around here because that's nothing but calling death." One night after curfew, they were out there playing, and I mean they was out there playing their little drums and marching. One of the little boys said, "Man, there's the police!" And he broke and ran! And another one of the little boys said, "Man you know you don't break the line for no police! You have to continue on with the band!" This is how some of these kids started Rebirth and Trombone Shorty! I remember how he used to be walking up and down with that trombone, and his mother would be right there with him.

During our construction of the community center, one of the contractors had bought some sixty-five drums for our youth and we had a young man who came over to teach them how to play. Man, Anne's daughter used to beat those drums. Now, we have a lot of programs. We have karate classes at least three times a week. We have a community dance, which is sponsored by the New Orleans Ballet Association. We have the after-school homework tutoring. We have the keyboard every Friday. We have the hip hop magazine. We have Men on the Move, which is a group of young men from Xavier [University] that's mentoring to our young boys.

Some community centers' hours are like from 8 in the morning 'til five in the evening. Not with us. We're here from sometimes twelve at night. We are here. And we're here for the people. We never know when a person gonna come in here and want something or they need some kind of information. We have to be here for them. The only time we like here real late is we've got a function going on and we have to get things together for the next day or whatever it is – but we as I said are here to serve the people. And its not about us. It's about how we serve others. And when we serving others, we serving God.

FLORENCE SLACK AND STELLA CARR, LONG-TERM MEMBERS OF THE RESIDENTIAL COUNCIL

FS: I remember we were living in the houses and had to move from there cuz they were building the projects. 24 something -

SC: 2432 Orleans. I remember that house.

FS: They told my dad we could move back in—he was a longshoreman.

SC: The development as a whole was very, very family-oriented. I had seven— five boys and two girls— and you know that was hard. My boys could bring other boys to the house, and those children respect me. If they did anything wrong – even on the outside – and you said, "Well, I'm going to tell your mother." Oh no, they didn't want you to do that! Because they knew what the outcome and the circumstances would be. See. That's what I liked about the resident council as a whole. They really work with those children [and] they really need it. They really need it.

FS: I wasn't on the board or anything like that, but being a resident in the projects, you try to become a part of it. You help in your own little way.

EC: They try to instill in our youth the things that they can do and they are behind them 100%. They had the little Lafitte Vikings. My son was in it. He played for basketball and baseball and all that. I think Dooky Chase had like a uniform for them and everything.

And they would take these children on trips and show them that there was another place – another way of life, take them to different places that they hadn't been before. This is interesting to them.

PART V: FRIENDS AND NEIGHBORS

When you grow up in public housing, you'll meet a lot of friends and have plenty more neighbors. Mainly because you grow up around the same people, you know their family and they know yours. You can't help but be cool with them. In this section, I reconnect with people I grew up around. It's full of pictures of people that when I first came around with my tape recorder and camera were about to have a panic attack, but they've since come around and gave the book just what it needed.

INTERVIEW WITH HOPE BLAND

Hope is one of the coolest people I've ever met. She's down to earth, funny, and would give you the clothes off her back if you asked her. As a child, I admired Hope. She was one of my best firends. I remember sleep-overs at her house with my brothers, sister, and cousin. We'd stay up late and play games like smut and pity pat. We'd watch movies. We really had fun with Hope. She has a generous heart and I can't think of anyone better to have my brother Willie's kids.

Hope: As a black female living in public housing, you already have stereotypes: You don't have anything. You're never going to be anything. You're just laying around, wasting up the government's time. Add to that being a woman and people look at you as though you're not supposed to have any sense. You're not supposed to know how to carry yourself. Your house is not supposed to be up to standards, you're not supposed to have any views, opinions, or know anything that matters.

When you do go out and be in the world, and tell someone your address, they look at you. A person who's livin in a house could be all the things that you expect for me to be, but because they're livin in a house or neighborhood [they aren't judged.] It be like that.

COMING OF AGE IN MISSISSIPPI

I grew up across the canal in the Lower Ninth Ward. I lived with my godmother since I was an infant. I was premature and my mother couldn't take care of me. She was still in my life, but I was just living with my godmother. I had a chance to go live with my mom, but I had been living with my nanna for so long, I just stayed with her.

We were very tight. Like daughter and mother should be. She wasn't my biological mother, but she was my mother in every other aspect. When I needed anything, she was there. She was a church-going person [and] a school teacher for twelve years. You know, she was just the absolute everything. She passed away March 7, this year. It was real unexpected for us.

Growing up, I was more or less like a tomboy. We didn't have uniforms then [in public school], so blue jeans, white t-shirt, and a French plait, that was my uniform for myself. Hair in a ponytail, everyday.

When I was fourteen up until sixteen and a half, I stayed with my aunt on this farm in Mississippi. It was great for me. I started evolving, put it like that. Instead of like looking at a boy and thinking, "Oh, that's my friend," I began to look at it like, "Well, he cute. I like him." Ya know what I'm saying? I think I got more girlfriend in Mississippi.

When I moved back to New Orleans, I stayed with my nanny up until I was seventeen. I moved out when I was pregnant. My nanny was okay with me livin there; I just wanted to get out and do it on my own. I was with the baby's father, so I moved with him. I was in my twelfth grade year in high school at George Washington Carver and I was working at Popeye's.

My nanny watched my little girl when I was in school. I only had like two classes. I went to school at ten o'clock and then I was off at eleven thirty. After I got outta school, I would go home and take care of my child. Then I would go to work for four till about eleven o'clock that night. It was a lot to juggle,

but it worked. It was my first real time seeing my name on a check ever in my entire life, so I was excited about that. Then I was going to prom and all kinds of stuff.

After I graduated, I moved up to a shift manager at Popeye's. I got a one bedroom for me and my daughter. I had already applied for a project and when [my daughter] was three weeks old, I applied for another one. A project didn't come up till she made three.

LAFITTE

I moved to an apartment in Lafitte on Orleans Avenue in 1999. My neighbors were all family. There was only one door on our porch we didn't associate with. In and out, you didn't have to lock your door. I had lost the key to my door for two whole years and never went and got another one.

I met Willie after living in Lafitte for about five months. He wasn't there when I first moved in. Where was he? He hadn't came home [until] July and we got together in August. His birthday is August the 8 and we got together the 16th. Ashley introduced us, so I have a vendetta against her for the rest of my life. [Laughing] In 2000, we had a little boy and [in] 2003, we had another little boy. I love him, that's my curse.

Willie Christopher George Nelson Mortry is different— put it like that. Sweet talker, big pretty puppy eyes. He's not a bad person. He'd give you the shirt off his back but you're going to have to do some fighting to get it. You really will. He has a rough side, and he has a tough side, and he has a mean side, and that's the side that he likes to show everybody. But underneath, when we're inside, the side that he keeps me close to him, he is really a very sweet person. Ashley will tell you, that's her brother.

Being in Lafitte and getting together with Willie was an eye opener. It really was. Because a lot of things that I didn't think I was groomed to, I was. And a lot of things that I didn't know, I had to learn real quick. And I learned it the hard way, over and over.

Here, they have such thing as a court. A court is where the projects are blocked in— there's no street that runs through em. And I had to learn that in those courts, that's where most of the people in the projects hang with their friends. Everyone goes outside. Your kids are out there. Certain courts have certain crowds. And within his crowd, Willie was popular because he grew up down there. The "in" thing for him was to go to the court. From my experience, when you have a girlfriend, we talk, we go to the show, we go out to eat, ya know, things that you would hope to do. His thing was, "You wanna see me, you come to the court with me."

I didn't know nothing about no court. The only

people I knew at that time was his family, which was Ashley and them. At that time, they were young. I'm like twenty-two, twenty-one, there's nothing we can talk about, ya know? Why would I go in the court with him, when I know no one in the court, and he's like popular? Everyone knows him. All the guys, they're talking, so there's nowhere for me to be, so I had to learn that.

We'd go through our problems. Right now, he's [in jail at Orleans Parish Prison on] Tulane and Broad. My children go and see him every Saturday. He'll be out in March. We've had our ups, we've had our downs, we've had our sideways, we've had our cross sideways, our triangles, our squares, and our octagons. I'm not going to say that it's the same anymore, but I love him. We're going through transition right now. We're more or less tryin to be friends. I have children for him—that's his only two boys, and it's my only two boys. So we're going to always have something special together.

I'd never take my children's daddy from them. I allow him to be their daddy as much as he can. When he messes up and he makes mistakes, I'm there. I'm on him, and he'll tell you that. I'm on him every step of that way. It's difficult because they're boys, and they want their daddy. They want someone to do the things that a daddy's supposed to do with their sons. And he's not there right now, ya know. But they love their daddy to death. They'd take their daddy over me, and I'm here everyday and he's not. In a way, I don't take that from him. I'd never take that from him.

LIVING ALONE

Everybody in this project—believe it or not—knows Hope, but Hope knows no one. And how they know Hope, that's through Willie. Because they know, "That's Willie's baby's mama." I only know people through "Oh that's such and such." or "That's so-and-so." But I don't know them as far as havin conversations or something like that.

This is my first time being in the court. I'm learnin. This is a brand new experience for me here. On the Avenue, your door is right there. If I was going to have company, my company could park their car right outside my door—just like a house or an apartment. As far as here, you probably have to come to the driveway and park out there. I'll give you another example. Cabs. I can get a cab on the Avenue like that. I can't get a cab in the court, because they're not coming to the driveway at night. At all, period. I guess it's the feel of actually having to come in the projects. The good have to suffer for the bad.

I'm working at Harrah's. Right now I cleanin up, but they want you to advance within. And they'll let people within advance faster than they will someone comin from the outside. The people on the outside get their chances to get in, but we get it first.

I'm trying to move out. My grandmother died on Mother's Day, so I'm trying to get her house in Jefferson Parish. That's goin to be a big step from here as far as being a home-owner.

INTERVIEW WITH CHARMAINE WILLIAMS

I remember going over to Ms. Charmaine's house and just having fun. She had three kids and they were all about my age. Wayman, Whitney, Tanya, Keitra, Domonique, and myself would all play hide n go seek, it, and other kinds of crazy games. Ms. Charmaine was cool, though, we'd make so much noise and she wouldn't even fuss.

She was good friends with my mom, and we've never lost touch. When she heard about me writing a book, she came by my grandma's to ask if she could be in it. Little did she know, she was already on the list for an interview. Ms. Charmaine is a real good person who has made it through the test of life. She has an open house where all are welcome. She's doing great and you can tell because she looks beautiful.

Ashley: Where did you grow up?

Charmaine: I grew up in the St. Bernard housing development, and the Ninth Ward, and the Seventh Ward. Now I'm in the Lafitte. I've been back here almost twenty years.

A: How did you move into public housing?

C: With some people, they say history repeat itself. I was unemployed. When I applied for my project, I had three choices: St. Bernard, Lafitte, or the Iberville. They gave me Lafitte, so I was good. It made me no difference. It was a home for me and my child.

A: And what do you like about the neighborhood?

C: The people. We're all family.

A: And do you have children in this neighborhood?

C: Yes I do. Children and grandchildren.

A: If you could tell someone about Lafitte, like describe it to them, what would you say?

C: It's a nice place to live. You know, it's like it's good and it's bad. But, it's how you live it; how you go through the good times and how you make it through the bad times. Like Ashley, and everybody around here, grew up together. Everybody's like one big family. And that's what makes it good. There's time things get rough and bad, but it's how we pull together to get through it.

Ashley's mother stayed right around the corner on Orleans. Yeah. And we was real good friends. We was real good friends. Her mom was a good person; a very good person. She went through it. We did a lot together. We did a lot of druggin together. I'm not ashamed of my past cuz my past made my future. It's who I am today. I'm a better person today. And I'm so proud of Ashley.

A: Thank you. What are some things that you're doing right now that you're enjoying and proud of?

C: I can do things now. We have parties, events come up. Everybody's always here for holidays. And I'm enjoying my grandchildren, all the children in the neighborhood. Everybody come by Ms. Charmaine.

INTERVIEW WITH PAT FULFORD

Ms. Pat is a respectful woman. She gives courtesy and expects it in return. She was real close friends with my mom. They grew up together in the same neighborhood and as kids hung together around the courts of Lafitte. Ms. Pat had similar struggles as my mom, but she's gotten through them. She says, "You gotta crawl before you can walk."

She's been working with HANO's Lafitte Beautification Crew since 1995. I remember when I was young, Ms. Pat was always working in the Lafitte. On and off duty, if she saw you throwing trash on the ground, she was making you pick it up. She takes pride in her job. She always makes sure the Avenue is clean and that people properly throw trash away.

She's highly involved in the community and always knows when the campaigning jobs are coming. She got me on a few times passing out papers for politicians around town.

Ashley: Where did you grow up?

Pat: Sixth Ward: Dumaine and Galvez. Originally? Governor Nicholls and Marais.

A: And how long have you been a part of this community?

P: I was seven years old when we moved here. I'll be forty in July, so it's been more than thirty years I've been a part of the Lafitte Housing Projects.

A: And what do you like about this neighborhood?

P: The change within it; how it's becoming now for the youngsters. The kids can play a little more now. It's not all—how I can say that? The violence.

A: Yeah. All right. And do you have children in this neighborhood?

P: Four kids. Two girls, two boys.

A: And, could you tell me like a story that happened on this block – something good, something bad, anything?

P: Everything is good, long as you keep your freedom. Do not get locked up. Do not get caught up in the drug game. Do not do dope. Play with the kids, you got a better chance of being a kid when you're an adult.

A: And if you could tell someone about Lafitte what would you say?

P: Great place to live to get a start, but if you have something to push out, get out. If you have teenagers, it's best if you can push out. And just don't lay low—meaning, lay low or stay and hang—just because you paying the free rent. Push out if you're a woman. You can make it yourself. I'm pushing out in two more months.

A: That's all good.

P: On my own, with a big yard. I'm a grandmother now, too! It's time to go.

A: Why did you move to Lafitte?

P: Well, my mom and dad didn't have no money. My mama never worked. My daddy always worked to put the food on the table and bought the clothes and paid all the bills. When they moved in the Lafitte Housing Projects, she got her first job at Travelodge Hotel at Canal and Claiborne, so I'm looking at 1974. She began working and he drove the school bus.

Ashley's mama was known as my mama before she ever had children. She's three years older than me. My sister and her went to school together, but me and her found our friendship together. They used to call me her daughter. Then she gave birth to her son named Willie. Me, Willie, and Jalna was always together.

We'd go to City Park and we'd bring Willie and he'll jump on the swings. We was like kids, too. And what else? We would go to Armstrong Park. That was the best. Willie would run around and get in the water and we hop in the water with him like big kids.

The grandmother always said, "Little boy, what you doing in my house?" Cuz I had short hair. She pulled a cover from over me one time and thought I was a boy laying in bed with Jalna. I had to be, what—thirteen? And Jalna was a few years older. Yeah. "Get out my house!" Then she say, "Oh, that's Pat!"

We played cards but she never was a gambler. And both of us fell off on our deep end. I always spent time with children and nobody knew I used it. But I've been clean since October 16, 1991. And that's the best freedom. I found out all them years I was loving a man, there wasn't no love with that man.

I found myself doing the same thing this man was doing.

I pushed my children to the side for awhile to push myself back up. Went into recovery, got help, and I ain't never found it necessary, since then, to use drugs again.

The man came for twelve o'clock on October the 16th, 1991, but he couldn't find me. I'm not gonna lie. I was boarded up in my house. I smoked a $100 in stones. And the man caught up with me at four. I jumped in his car—yep. I stayed in rehab thirty days.

A: What about your job?

P: I did a lot of volunteer coming up and when I went to fill out the application, the lady told me no, she didn't need me. She wanted the man. She took the man and shut the door on me. I opened the door at 709 N. Galvez—I remember this good. October the 5th, 1995 – she shuts the door on me. I opened it back up. I said, "No! " She said, "We gonna just use you temporary." When I went to the HANO office on Carondelet Street, I was supposed to take [the] temporary but instead I took a permanent ID! And ever since then, I've been a member of the Lafitte Beautification Improvement.

Uncle Michelle: And they ain't cleaned up like her since!

P: I worked myself up to Orleans and Claiborne; then to a supervisor position in 2003. What a blessing.

INTERVIEW WITH JACKIE FULFORD

Ashley: How did you end up in this neighborhood?

Jackie: Well, let me see. I came here with my parents in 1974. I ended living up on 2430 Orleans avenue for seventeen years. I've been knowing Ashley Nelson since she was a baby. The house we was living in on Dumaine was condemned, we moved to the Lafitte Projects.

A: And what do you like about the neighborhood?

J: I like my neighbors on Orleans Avenue. They do look out for our children. They look for they people. And we all come as one. I've been on the Avenue so long, even though I've moved to Rocheblave, I sit there on the Avenue like I still live there.

A: Now can you give me a story, of neighbors sticking together?

J: Yeah. We have barbeques, parties. You know, everybody would pitch in. If they see your kids running in the street, they would look out for them.

A: Alright, you gotta give me a little story about when we was younger – oooh –

J: Look, I'm not gonna tell on you –

A: Everybody on the Avenue knew everybody on the Avenue.

J: The Nelson family was the little bad children. If you fight one, you had to fight em all. It wasn't no one man game. But you had to mess with em. And when you did, that's when they come out. You step on her toe—that was it.

A: You never thought I would be writing a book, Jackie though?

J: No, I would never thought this in a million years but I'm proud of you. And I'm glad to see somebody in the neighborhood do something good for the people back here.

INTERVIEW WITH WANDA DUBOUSE

Some people say Ms. Wanda is kinda throwed off because she has a dog that's a hundred years old, but in my opinion she's one of the sanest people I know. Ms. Wanda is giving, and that alone says a lot. She lived next door to me for as long as I can remember and used to babysit us when my parents went to work. We'd all sit in the living room and watch TV or listen to her sing. She has a beautiful voice that draws you in. She sang old goodies and my personal favorites—the song from the movie The Color Purple, "Sista" and "God Is Trying to Tell You Something." She would sound just as good or even better than Shug Avery. Still, to this day if my sista Keitra and I see Ms. Wanda going to the store or anywhere, we'll stop her and beg her to sing to us because we grew up on that voice. Ms. Wanda was more than a neighbor to us. She was like an aunt. I know we drove her crazy, but she watched us anyway.

EARLY YEARS

I was born at 1622 Orleans Street in the Seventh Ward. My father was a laborer; my mother was a housewife. I'm the youngest of six: four boys and two girls. In the Seventh Ward it was Indians. It was about Mardi Gras, St. Joseph's, and stuff where all the Indians would come out. Parents would be cooking suppers. My girlfriend's daddy was a musician, and they used to rehearse for the band. We would sit out there and listen. One guy would get out there and do the James Brown. I really miss that part of my life.

Ashley: Go ahead, girl. How long have you lived your life in Lafitte?

W: Approximately 37 years. I came to Lafitte housing project at the age of 14. My father had passed over. Back then times was hard. By my mama being a homemaker, she didn't have the money to pay the rent, and so she applied for assistance for emergency housing. And, that's how I wind up becoming a native in the Lafitte housing.

A: What was the Lafitte like back then?

W: Oh, God, it was beautiful.

A: It was beautiful?

W: Trees — I mean, it was like City Park. It was party time. Barbeques, birthday parties, all the neighbors in the street — wasn't no violence. None whatsoever. Everybody's child was everybody's child. Ashley was my child. I raised her from a baby. I used to rub her mommy's stomach when she was carrying her. And all the rest of em.

When her momma moved back here, she just had Willie and Keitra. That was the only two. So I raised every last one of them. When her mama would go to work, I would watch em. Put em in the living room, and you sit down there, play on the top porch, they'd do their little work and stuff. I then raised so many of these children around here, I think I could be on welfare.

A: And the little parakeet y'all had in the kitchen —

W: I had a little parakeet named Tweety Bird. And we enjoyed ourself. Life was sweet.

Ashley's mom would tell everybody I was her sister. She used to be in my house, I'd be in her house. We'd sit out on the porch with crawfish. She disciplined her kids. Oh yes, they were gonna get theirs.

A: You disrespect, oh no —

W: If I come and tell them — she gonna get on them. Mmhmm. Oh yeah. Sometimes I wouldn't even speak to em, I'd be so mad with them. But I love em.

CHANGES

A: You talk about the Lafitte back then, how do you think it's changed now?

W: Oh my God, it's hard to describe. It really is. When we was coming up, you could chastise somebody's child. Now, the children call the police on you. So, you more or less back off. You're afraid to speak out because of the drugs. You more or less be quiet.

A: You shut up.

W: Nobody wants to get their house shot up and no-

body wants to get shot up. It's not like it used to be. And to be honest with you, it's a damn shame. You can't even sit on your porch; you'll be harassed by the police.

A: Yeah. That's right.

W: If you walk out of your door and you don't have an ID on you, you going to jail.

A: You going straight to jail.

W: For trespassing. And this is where you live at. They stop you for nothing. They know who they looking for. Why stop the ones that you know that's not doing anything? Grab the ones that's doing it.

A: Mmmhmm.

W: Maybe we could come back to the trees and the palm trees and the nightwatch. People could sit out on their porch and eat crawfish and drink their beer like they used to.

A: What do you see in this neighborhood?

W: Death.

A: Death? What you mean?

W: You never know when a bullet gonna come through your window. Or you never know when you gonna walk out the door and never walk back in.

A: Do you feel safe here?

W: Honestly speaking?

A: Yes.

W: No I don't. Not anymore.

A: Yeah, a lot of people have been getting killed.

W: It's like Death Valley. It really is. It's a war zone. Many nights when I hit the floor. AK-47's, Uzi's, Street Sweepers. You never know when somebody gonna blow a hole through your door.

The thing about back here, we do stick together. Especially when somebody dies. Everybody laughs, everybody cries. You know? But why we keep killing each other? There's no reason. Because I don't have Nikes, you want my tennies? I don't have Reeboks. I don't have a name brand jacket, shoes, pants, that stuff?

Why you don't like me? Not that it matters. Because I'm still gonna give you the time of the day. When we was coming up, you don't never walk by somebody and don't speak to them: "Oh no, you didn't speak to Ms. So-and-so? Let's go. We going back down there." You don't walk away from elders. These kids today, look dead in your face—

A: And just walk straight past you.

W: And walk straight past you. Mother f'er this!

A: They've gone crazy.

W: And some of the women really need to get their mind right and stop letting the little guys come in their house and sell drugs. When they get busted, they get put out. You on the street, not him! They then made their money off of you. They get your nails done. They get your hair done. Buy you a pair of jewels. [But] when the man come through that door, or kick it down, where you going at? Nowhere.

Don't think cuz somebody tell you they love you they mean it. They might like you. But what they gonna do? I'm a woman. I know. I've been there. I've been through the wringer, Ashley, and you know that. Really. But believe you me, you don't have to worry about me coming back with nobody to the house no more. That's the thing about it. I know where I've been, but they still don't know where they're going.

Basically, you're not safe in your own home. Your friends are not your friends anymore. I'll put it to you like that. People that you've been knowing for years, their life has changed tremendously. Because of the drugs. And you don't know who to trust. So, you try to shut it out. Basically, that's what I have done. It's all right to come to my house. But I want you out of my house at a certain time. I still love you, and I respect you. But you don't respect my home.

This is the only home that I have right about now. As a matter of fact, I have nobody else; my mother's in the aged home.

A: What about your other family?

W: One of my brothers lives in California, one lives in Texas, one lives in Baton Rouge, and my sister lives in the East. When my momma took sick, I wound up back in the projects to take care of her. I was out of here for about eight or nine years.

NIGHTCLUBS

A: Let me tell you something about Ms. Wanda. She is a snappy dresser. Ms. Wanda know how to dress. She got some clothes and some hats and some shoes that are pink, purple and all that -

W: You like my clothes?

A: Yes, you got some —

W: Well thank you.

A: Oh yeah. You got a thing for *The Color Purple*. After the interview, you gotta sing that song. She used to sing in——

W: I used to sing in nightclubs. But I ain't doing no singing. One of the band members is sick, but if they find somebody and they have an opening somewhere (snap)…I'll be there.

A STORY ABOUT LAFITTE

A: You gotta tell me a story of something that happened in Lafitte – good, bad, anything. Just a good story.

W: A good story. Oh. I had a friend, she was like a

sister to me, and I loved her very, very dearly. She had eight children. And all of them was my babies. And now they all grown. But she left. The Lord said it was time for her to come home. Her name was Jalna Nelson. And that's where you came from. And I love you very much.

A: I love you too, Ms. Wanda.

W: And I'm glad you're here with me today. You take care of yourself and you be safe and you be strong. And whatever you achieve today in life makes your mama so happy. Keep a smile. Dream on baby, dream on. And that's my story.

A: My mama, she was a stallion.

W: She was a brickhouse, baby. Oh yeah. She's a real fine woman. You see all the kids she had? She was a very beautiful woman. She got along with everybody. She was good people, you know. When she passed on, I don't know, look like everything I touched, I loved, just fade away. But I always keep her in my heart. She was a lady, regardless of what anybody would say about her. It's what in her heart that counts. And she had a heart.

CONCLUSION: MY BROTHER IS HOME!!!

It was early Easter Sunday morning when I first heard my cell phone ringing. I hate waking up. Sometimes I wish I could sleep forever because the dream world is so much easier than the real world. Anyway, I woke up and opened the phone and saw that it was my grandma who called. I checked my call log and her number came up at least twelve times. I called back, but as usual, no one answered. After trying a few more times Anthony answered. I asked him if anyone had called my phone and he said it might have been Willie.

My grandma told me Willie was coming home on Easter but I thought it would be night-time. I was happy to know he was home again. He'd been in jail for two years and I missed him. After I hung up with Anthony, I told my younger brothers and sisters who already knew. I had just slept a little late and was the last in the family to know.

My dad brought all of us across the river to see him at my grandma's house. Everyone gave him hugs and talked to him. He told us he wanted to get a job and support his boys. And he did. He's doing construction work and staying out of trouble. He plans on getting married to a young lady he met while he was in prison. My brother is home, Willie's back— however you say it, he still here.

PROVIDENCE CEMETERY

THE REASON I DID NOT CRY

It's my first day back since January 10, 2001. It looks different, but still hurts. It's been almost five years since I've been back, and I feel ashamed I've been gone so long, but you know what? I'm glad I came. I guess I avoided coming back because my fear of the place. Graveyards aren't my favorite place to be and being there visiting my mother made it worse. But I didn't cry. I refused to cry. I've cried for too many years. I was here now only to be strong and visit the place where my mom's body is at peace.

When I decided to go, I called my grandma's house to see who was there and who wanted to come. When I asked Keitra, she said, "Fuckin right. Let's go." Willie just said yes. When we arrived at the site, I told myself before getting out of the car: *Do not cry! Please, Ashley, don't because that will make it harder.* We all walked over to the plot and just stood there looking up.

There was nothing but silence for the first fifteen minutes, and that's how it should have been. I don't know what was on Willie and Keitra's mind, but all I could think about was how proud my mom would be if she could be here with us now. Willie's out of jail, working and taking care of kids. He's planning on getting married soon. Keitra has a beautiful daughter. She's working now and plans to go back to school. Domonique also has a beautiful daughter and is still one of the best rappers I've ever heard. Bigman is going to school, working and, getting on my nerves. Mikky is trying and she always told us that if you at least try you might just get somewhere. And Jenny and Nuder are both making good grades and touching less of my stuff.

When I left the cemetery, I felt this feeling of relief, which made me happy. I mean, I love my mom and would give anything to have her back, but I can't. All I can do is accept the truth that she's gone and I am here. I know her memory will live in my family and me because we love her. This year while I was working on my book, I realized she lives on in Lafitte, too. As I walked down the Ave. or through the courts, people said, "You Jalna's daughter, huh?" I always raised my head and said, "Yes," because I proud to be a part of her. And though the loss was heartbreaking, her memory keeps me going. This is the reason I did not cry.

118

THE NEIGHBORHOOD STORY PROJECT
OUR STORIES TOLD BY US

What you have just read is one of the five books to come from the first year of the Neighborhood Story Project. This has been an incredible year for us, and we thank you for your support and attention.

The Neighborhood Story Project would like to give a big shout out to the people of the City of New Orleans—y'all are the best. Thank you for showing so much love.

There are lots of folks and organizations that have made this possible. You have come through with stories, with food, with love, and with money—and believe us when we say that all four are necessary.

First off, we'd like to acknowledge our great partners, the Literacy Alliance of Greater New Orleans and the University of New Orleans. Specifically, Peg Reese, Rachel Nicolosi, Rick Barton, Tim Joder, Bob Cashner, Susan Krantz and Jeffrey Ehrenreich have been excellent supervisors and colleagues.

To Steve Gleason and Josselyn Miller at the One Sweet World Foundation. Thank-you for getting this project from the very beginning, and for having such awesome follow through.

To the institutions of the city that have been good to us—thank you. Good institutions play such an important role in making a place. Specifically we'd like to thank the Greater New Orleans Foundation, The Lupin Foundation, The Louisiana Endowment for the Humanities, Tulane Service Learning, The Schweser Family Foundation, and the guys from the Cultivating Community Program for donating the proceeds from your work with Longue Vue to help us get these books out.

To all of the individuals who have stepped up and given so much—from the donation of stamps to all the folks who have trusted us with their money. To Phyllis Sassoon and Mick Abraham for donating their cars. To all the folks who contributed, from the change jars at Whole Foods to the checks and food donations.

Thanks to our incredible steering committee, GK Darby, Peter Cook, Norbert Estrella, Tim Lupin, and Eliza Wells.

To Kalamu ya Salaam and Jim Randels at SAC, for taking us in and showing us the ropes, and giving us support as we try to grow. If we have done anything right as teachers it is because you have taught us.

To the administration of John McDonogh Senior High, Principal Spencer, and the past principals Winfield and Goodwin, thank you for being such great partners. To Ms. Pratcher and Ms. Tuckerson, thank you and bless you for dealing with all the headaches we cause. And to the staff at John McDonogh, we are so proud to be working with you.

To Elena Reeves and Kenneth Robin at the Tchopshop, thanks for being great designers, and for being such great sports about working with us. And to Jenny LeBlanc and Kyle Bravo at Hot Iron Press, thank you for being great designers/printer and for moving to town.

To Lauren Schug and Heather Booth, for transcribing and transcribing, above and beyond the call of duty.

To Anita Yesho for copy editing at short notice.

To Stephanie Oberhoff, and Communities in Schools- your mission is beautiful and your execution is great.

To Beverly McKenna, thank you for giving us such a beautiful office when we were only a sliver of an idea.

To Gareth Breunlin, who laid out the books and designed the covers. You have made our ideas come out on paper in a way that has honored all of the work and love involved.

To Davey and Jamie for being our dogs.

To Jerry for grant-writing, copy-editing, and being our hero.

To Dan, for his constant input, sharing a car and a computer, writing grants and cooking numerous dinners for the NSP.

To Shana, for promoting this project like it was your own, and for the input and help and grace.

And our biggest thank-you and respect to all of the Bolding, Jackson, Nelson, Price, and Wylie families. Without your love and care, this would not have been possible. Thank you for believing in the project and the work, and for making these books what they are.

And to Palmyra, Lafitte, St. Claude, Dorgenois (and the rest of Ebony's Sixth Ward), and N. Miro, thank you for your stories. We hope you like the books as much we liked making them.

The list is so long because so many of you have contributed.

Thanks for reading.

For the Neighborhood Story Project

Rachel Breunlin
Abram Himelstein

P.S. Thank you to Richard Nash, Ammi Emergency and Soft Skull Press for believing in us and New Orleans in our time of need.